ACE

& PROUD

& PROUD

An Asexual Anthology

Edited by
A.K. Andrews

ACE & PROUD: AN ASEXUAL ANTHOLOGY

Copyright ©2015 by Purple Cake Press
ISBN-13: 978-1517286668
ISBN-10: 1517286662
1st Edition

Collected and edited by A.K. Andrews

Ace & Proud: An Asexual Anthology is available online and in print. Please ask your local library and bookstore to stock it.

This book is dedicated to everyone
who has ever felt ...

abnormal
unnatural
incomplete
ashamed
invisible
broken

You are none of these things.
You are not alone.
And you are loved.

Table of Contents

1   Foreword
Victoria Beth

4   Introduction
A.K. Andrews

10   Glossary

12   My Self-discovery, Thus Far
Rebecca Nesor

17   A Geeky Love Story
Suma

23   Growing Up
Phil Dalton

32   Coming Out
Melissa Keller

37   Being "Normal" is Overrated Anyway
Ren

43   Finding Grace
Betty Badinbed

58   Black Women Can Be Asexual Too
Gabriella Grange

64   Fixing What Isn't Broken
Emma Hopwood

67   I Just Don't Get It
      Jennifer Dyse

70   An Asexual Teen
      Kaya Brown

75   Dream Guy
      Cionii

77   It's All Asexual To Me
      Jarrah Shub

82   When I Grow Up
      Shannon Brown

86   Just A Small Town Boy
      Cameron

90   Coming Out To Myself: Not A Piece Of Cake
      Ennis

Foreword
Victoria Beth (AVEN Project Team)

When Alfred Kinsey set out to document the sexual experiences of America's population in the mid-20th century, little did he or the rest of the world anticipate some of his findings. His "Kinsey Scale"—introduced in the book *Sexual Behaviour in the Human Male* (1948), and drawn on again in *Sexual Behaviour in the Human Female* (1953)—graded sexuality on a 0-6 scale, with 0 being fully heterosexual and 6 being fully homosexual. The Kinsey Scale also introduced the concept of a person who experienced no socio-sexual contacts or reactions, represented on the scale as an 'X'. One of the first academic acknowledgements of asexuality had been made, and this paved the way for more research into a field that had gone largely unstudied for most of history.

At the dawn of the new millennium, an asexual community began to grow—due in no small part to the increasing use of the internet and the founding of the Asexual Visibility and Education Network (AVEN) in 2001 by David Jay. AVEN served as a vital platform for asexual people to meet, discuss, seek advice, and plan visibility efforts, eventually becoming the largest online asexuality resource and often the first point of contact people had with the asexual community. By 2009, AVEN members were representing asexuality for the first time in pride events like the San Francisco Pride Parade.

Today, AVEN has over 100,000 active members from both the English site and alternate language AVEN forums. It is the largest online asexual forum, and is now an official Non-Profit Organization. Its members frequently appear in pride events, organize meetups, and publish visibility-related materials and news stories. On the forums and in the chatroom, projects such as this one are organized, support is offered to those in need, and stories are exchanged.

In this anthology, AVEN's role in the asexual community is clear. For many of the authors, it was the place they first found a community of people who could understand them and their experiences, the place that put into words

mostly fabricated and/or exaggerated. It was only after entering a sexual relationship with a boy that I started to think something might be different about *me*. The lightbulb moment came when I discovered asexuality in a blog post. I joined AVEN soon after, eventually becoming a member of the Project Team in order to get better involved in asexuality visibility efforts.

Everyone in the asexual community has a story to tell, and it is through sharing these stories that we can gain a greater understanding of each other and achieve greater awareness in the wider population. So sit back, relax, and enjoy a selection of personal experiences, insights, and anecdotes from asexual writers around the world!

Introduction

A.K. Andrews

"An asexual is someone who does not experience sexual attraction. Unlike celibacy, which people choose, asexuality is an intrinsic part of who we are."

– AVEN website

Imagine that you live in a world where everyone is obsessed with pie. The lyrics to every Top 10 song either revolve around the acquisition of pie, the consumption of pie, or heartbreak over lack of pie. Teenagers in high school classrooms can barely focus on their schoolwork because they're busy fantasizing about eating pie. Poets write odes to pie, and beautiful

[text obscured]

once or twice out of curiosity, although the experience wasn't exactly satisfying. You know that most people look at pie and feel an overwhelming urge to consume it, but you feel nothing. It's just pie, for heaven's sake! What's all the fuss about?

Now replace pie with sex, and you've just peeked into the mind of an asexual (or, "ace") person. It's not a perfect analogy, obviously, but I think you get the picture.

A lot of people believe that asexuality isn't real. They argue that disinterest in sex isn't a natural condition, but rather a medical issue that requires treatment, or a psychological problem caused by childhood trauma. But asexuality is very real, and it's not a problem that needs to be overcome—it's a sexual orientation, just like heterosexuality, homosexuality, or bisexuality. And it's not as uncommon as you might think. Recent studies estimate that one person in every hundred is asexual—meaning that, with a world population of over seven billion, there are approximately 70 million asexuals alive today.

But despite this huge number of asexual people, you rarely hear about asexuality. That's because it's not an issue that's really on the public radar yet. And that makes a lot of sense, because whereas something like gay marriage causes a lot of controversy and attracts a lot of media attention, there aren't really any controversial subjects surrounding asexuality.

Ever so slowly, though, asexual awareness and visibility is increasing. It's happening through word of mouth, through a handful of asexual characters popping up on TV (like Sheldon Cooper from *The Big*

Bang Theory, or the titular protagonist of *Dexter*), through the hard work and dedication of organizations like the Asexual Visibility and Education Network (AVEN), and through projects like this anthology. It's going to take time, but we're all working toward creating a world where everyone knows that asexuality exists—toward creating a world where no one will have to spend years thinking they're "broken" because they don't want to have sex and don't understand why they feel that way.

This anthology began the way many passion projects do—I went looking for something, couldn't find it, and decided to create it myself. In this case, I was looking for a book containing a collection of personal essays about asexuality; stories from real asexual people about real life experiences that I could identify with, empathize with, and learn

In the pages of this anthology, you'll find 17 autobiographical stories from asexual writers around the world. (Note that some of the writers have chosen to use pen names in order to preserve their anonymity.) These stories are:

My Self-discovery, Thus Far – Rebecca Nesor shares her experience as a 21st century asexual teenager, which involves an amusing anecdote about phone shopping and Minecraft.

A Geeky Love Story – Suma walks us through the romantic tale of how sie joined a comics group looking for friendship and good times, and ended up falling in love.

Growing Up – Phil Dalton offers a series of vignettes stretching over 30 years, from his childhood to the present day, about his attempts to fit into a sexual society.

Coming Out – Melissa Keller explains why she has chosen not to come out to her friends and family, and explores the struggles that many asexual people face when coming out.

Being "Normal" Is Overrated Anyway – Ren describes how she discovered she wasn't as "normal" as she'd thought, and how she's come to embrace her asexuality.

Finding Grace – Betty Badinbed reflects on the 20+ years of relationships—brief and lengthy, platonic and romantic, failed and successful—which have helped her hone her gray-ace identity.

Black Women Can Be Asexual Too – Gabriella Grange explores her experiences as a black asexual young woman, including a sweet story about a handsome cellist and their shared passion for philosophy.

Fixing What Isn't Broken – Emma Hopwood shares a humorous piece of prose poetry about how tough it is to be asexual in a sexual world.

I Just Don't Get It – Jennifer Dyse offers insight into how hard it is to navigate school and relationships as an asexual, and the dangers that can come from trying too hard to be "normal."

An Asexual Teen – Kaya Brown ruminates on her experiences as an asexual teen, on coming out to her mother, and on dealing with distrust from adults who don't understand asexuality.

Dream Guy – Cionii shares a poem about inner beauty.

It's All Asexual To Me –

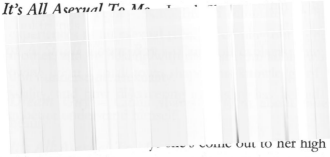

come out to her high school friends.

Just A Small Town Boy – Cameron explains how growing up in a small town shaped his knowledge of sexuality, and how discovering asexuality has helped him better understand himself.

Coming Out To Myself: Not A Piece Of Cake – Ennis discusses her journey, as a young lady with Asperger's syndrome, toward accepting her aromantic and asexual identity.

Copper Weddings – Martin Spangsbro-Pedersen explains why he cast off his gay identity to instead identify as asexual, and describes his experiences as an activist within Denmark's LGBTQ+ community.

My Happily Ever After – Cecily Summers explains how her definition of her own "happily ever after" changed after she identified herself as asexual.

As you can see, this anthology offers a wide variety of stories on a wide variety of topics. Whether you're a newly-discovered asexual, someone who's known they're asexual for years, the friend or family of someone asexual, or someone who's just intrigued by asexuality in general, you're sure to find something here that interests you. And if you find yourself confused by any of the terms used in the anthology, please consult the Glossary for definitions.

It has been my honor and pleasure to collect, polish, and publish these pieces. I hope you'll enjoy reading them just as much as I have, and will walk away with a better understanding of the sexual spectrum of the human race!

Glossary

Ace / Asexual – someone who does not experience sexual attraction to others

Aromantic – someone who does not experience romantic attraction to others

AVEN – the Asexual Visibility and Education Network, a non-profit organization focused on creating public awareness of asexuality and growing an asexual community

Cis / Cisgender – someone who identifies as the gender they were assigned at birth

Demiromantic – someone who only experiences romantic attraction after first forming an emotional connection

someone who is sexually attracted to the opposite gender

Homosexual – someone who is sexually attracted to the same gender

Kinsey Scale – the Heterosexual-Homosexual Rating Scale, developed by Alfred Kinsey, which grades sexuality on a 0-6 scale (0 being fully heterosexual, 6 being fully homosexual); asexuality is represented as "X"

LGBTQ+ – acronym meaning Lesbian, Gay, Bisexual, Transgender, and Questioning (the plus sign stands for all sexual identities not covered in the acronym, including asexuality)

Non-binary / Genderqueer – someone who identifies as neither, both, or a combination of male and female genders

Sie / Hir / Hirs – pronouns for a non-binary / genderqueer person

My Self-discovery, Thus Far

Rebecca Nesor

Rebecca Nesor was born in 1997 in New Jersey. She enjoys playing the clarinet and engaging in other musical activities. She also enjoys reading and making videos.

When I was a freshman in high school, someone asked me if I was gay. Harmlessly, in math class, over geometry problems.

"No, no," I said quickly. I'm sure I was the color of a bright tomato.

"Really?" the person replied. "You lik~~~~~

~~~~~~

~~~~~t~~ like a girl, either. I never had.

When I went home that day, I decided to convince myself that I was straight. Since I had never shown any preference toward either sex, might as well choose the "easy" one, right? I decided that I would have to like someone. My boy of choice was Phil of the Future, simply because I had found the entire show on YouTube earlier in the week and was watching it anyway. Besides, Phil of the Future was pretty cute. However, within a week I'd grown bored of looking at videos of Phil of the Future. I'd watched the whole show and realized that he was *significantly* less interesting without his time machine and sprayable brownies. I decided I needed a new target for my affections.

My new target was a cute boy in my history class, who had just switched into our school midway through the year. He sat in the back row, and I sat in the front. I made a conscious decision to have a crush on him, and I spent his first day in class turning around many times to look at him. This was a calculated move—I had determined that if I turned around enough times, I would suddenly like him. The problem with this plan was that I forgot to turn around and look at him the next day in class. And then I forgot every day after that. When I remembered my plan months later, I realized I needed to go back to the drawing board.

Since the "try to be straight" thing wasn't working, 15-year-old me decided the next logical step was to learn more about gay people. My medium of choice was YouTube, on my phone, wearing headphones as I watched videos in my bed in the middle of the night. I didn't know where to start, so I literally searched "gay." I tried to watch as many videos as I could, and after watching shows like *Gay Family Values* and *Kaelyn and Lucy,* I came away with a new conclusion: I wasn't gay. At least, not really. I liked watching gay couples because I thought they were cuter, generally, than straight couples. But part of my preference for gay couples was just that I was tired of watching a boy and girl fall in love on TV—it got boring after a while, the same old thing over and over.

I became confused and frustrated, because I didn't know what I was. Maybe there was something wrong with me? I even wondered if I was an alien at one point. Nothing else seemed to make sense.

As a high school sophomore, I tried my hardest to look interested when my friends gushed about celebrity

I don't remember when it was exactly that I first learned about asexuality. It was at some point relatively early on in my junior year. Mostly likely I saw it mentioned on Tumblr, a site where I had just begun to become active. I tried looking for more information about asexuality on YouTube (my old go-to), but found pretty much nothing, so I switched to Tumblr. And what I found there was better than I had hoped for—real people explaining what asexuality was, and what it meant to them.

As I scrolled along, I discovered there was an online asexual community. It was small, and vastly underrepresented in the media, but the most important thing was that I was not alone. There were other people like me out there who were experiencing the same thing as I was.

Tumblr led me to AVEN and to other sites that defined and explained asexuality. I Googled and researched and read and learned, and came away from the experience feeling a sense of elation that I realized I hadn't felt in a long time. I wasn't alone. There was nothing wrong with me.

The asexual flag is black and grey and white and purple. As someone who *only* wears those colors, the whole thing seemed magical, like it was meant to be. I tried to wear all of those colors the day after I embraced my asexuality, to quietly represent my ace pride.

I distinctly remember that a few weeks after I realized I was asexual, my mom, my sister, and I went to the Verizon store to pick up a new phone for my sister. In the many hours we had to wait for someone to help us, I stood over a sample iPad with the trial version of Minecraft on it and used it to build an asexual flag. Giant stripes of black and grey and white and purple, hidden deep in a pixelated world. I sometimes wonder if anyone ever found it—and if they did, I wonder if they knew what it meant.

It's been two years since then. I've barely told anyone that I'm asexual. When I was a junior, one of my best friends asked me how I identified, and I told him. He's awesome and he doesn't care at all, and will occasionally send me ace puns over Tumblr. I've told my sister. I've told my parents—and while my dad is totally accepting of it, my mom insists I'll "grow out of it." I'm working on trying to educate and convince her.

I'm still young. I haven't figured out a romantic orientation that suits me yet. I'm sure that will evolve

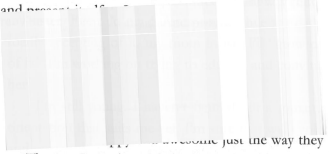

are. The way I am. Asexual. And proud.

A Geeky Love Story

Suma

Suma is a non-binary person from Scotland who spends far too much time getting distracted by TV shows and comic books when sie should be studying for a Physics degree. Sie has somehow surrounded hirself with the queerest gang of fellow physicists known to humanity, and is really suffering from cat withdrawal symptoms.

I've known I was asexual since I was 12. It was never a question for me—it just made sense, and I embraced it as part of who I was.

A few years later, I was basically told by my first serious crush that he wouldn't consider dating someone "like me." At that point, I pretty much gave up on ever finding someone non-asexual to be in a relationship with. I won't lie—I was devastated. So, I did what I've always done when my emotions get to be too much: I stuck them in a little box, locked it up, and threw away the key. As a rather cynical demiromantic, I figured I would either somehow meet another asexual person by chance, or else live a life without romance—which, admittedly, was part of my life plan since age 12 anyway.

17

So when I, geek that I am, went to the small comics group set up in my local library, I fully expected to spend the evening arguing over who would win in a fight between Squirrel Girl and Elastic Man (Squirrel Girl every time!), and discussing whether the new Marvel film was true to the comics. Making a few new friends along the way would be great. Romance, though, never crossed my mind.

I got on pretty well with everyone—the comics group turned out to be a close-knit group of friends, and I felt perfectly comfortable hanging out with and coming out to them.

I also hit it off with one guy in particular who came each week. So, when the person he usually went to the cinema with bailed, it seemed like common sense for him to invite me along in their place. For me it was just a f

"So, older than you, then?"

"We're *not* going on a date."

"So, did you enjoy your date?"

"IT WASN'T A DATE!"

This continued for some time after we'd been to the cinema. I mostly ignored it, and he and I continued on as usual—we'd meet every second Wednesday and argue about comics and TV and anything else we could think of, and occasionally we'd engage in snark warfare over Facebook or text.

Then I went to London for a week to do an exhibition with my school. He spent the first two days complaining via text about having to go to Glasgow Comic Con on his own. I responded with photos of a dinosaur skeleton, and gloated about seeing the helmet Karl Urban wore as Judge Dredd (yes, we are honestly that geeky). We ended up chatting well past midnight every night, and by the end of the week, pretty much everyone at the exhibition was sure he was my boyfriend.

We kept chatting incessantly over the summer, work allowing. Whenever I got a lift home after a late shift at work, he was the one I let know that I'd arrived home safely. We went to the cinema, snarked some more, went to a small Comic Con with some others from the group …

And then I moved away to university. We promised we'd keep in touch, and we spent most of the first few days I was in Glasgow exchanging our usual snarky messages. Then, midweek, everything changed.

I went to a society meet-up and chatted with a guy about anime—which isn't really my thing, but after hanging around with a few ridiculously huge anime and manga fans, you pick things up. Anime Guy asked if I wanted to meet up before the society lunch the next day, and I blithely (with the social-awareness of a sheltered demiromantic) said yes. It was only later that night that my brain kicked in and went, "Wait, was he asking me on a *date?*"

Needing a second opinion, I texted my guy friend—my cinema buddy, my snark friend, the guy everyone kept mistaking for my boyfriend—for advice. I described the situation and asked him if I'd just been asked out on a date. After 20 minutes of radio silence, he finally responded with the message: "I like you."

car so he could walk around the park and freak out over the thought of me going on a date with someone else. He'd then gotten back into the car and asked one of the comics group guys for help, who'd typed the "I like you" message into his phone. He'd accidentally hit send when they handed his phone back, whilst saying "I can't send that!" When I'd responded that I needed time to think about what he'd said, that phone was allegedly flung at a tree.

So, after a week and a half of awkward talks through texting and Facebook, we were finally face-to-face again. I opened with a pun, since he tends to enjoy puns to an insanely bad degree. Finally, after three and a half hours of talking—admittedly, we did keep getting distracted with other stuff—we decided to give a romantic relationship a shot.

Our first date consisted of watching Doctor Who and then going comic shopping. I think it worked out quite well.

The relationship is mostly long-distance, with us meeting up for one day every two or three weeks. Our weekends together usually involve snuggling up and watching TV shows in bed. Slowly—very, very slowly—we've started getting more physical. I never feel pressured. I never feel like he'll get upset if I say, "Stop." I'm not sex-repulsed, but I also don't have much of a libido. If you told me tomorrow I couldn't have sex ever again, I'd probably shrug and move on. But I know sex means something to him, and therefore it means something to me, because I care about him.

I always get scared when people tell me nightmare stories of everything that can go wrong in a relationship between an asexual person and a sexual person. I suppose it's because everything in my own relationship seems to be going so perfectly—I'm terrified that it'll go wrong at a moment's notice. Yet at the same time I know it won't, because he accepts me for who I am, and for what I am. And that is amazing.

Growing Up

Phil Dalton

Phil Dalton is in his 30s, from Ireland, and writes in his spare time from work and general procrastination. He has been in the middle of writing a novel for the last 18 months. One day it will be finished. Hopefully.

Age 6

I've been in school for one year now, learning and playing, although usually just by myself or with my imaginary friends because I've struggled to make real friends. I don't have a bad relationship with anyone in my class—I just don't have any relationship with them at all. Despite having two brothers, I tend not to mix well with other kids. Not like Ben, who got the entire class to come to his 7th birthday party. I wish I could be more like Ben, but I'm not, and I don't know how to change that.

Age 9

Every fortnight, my family and I visit my maternal grandparents, who live an hour away. Every fortnight, my grandmother has the same question for me: "Have you got a girlfriend yet?" And every fortnight,

I cringe with embarrassment and respond: "I have friends that are girls, but no girlfriends."

The use of plural in "friends" is a lie, of course—I have only one female friend who I can talk to and get on with. Her name is Rebecca. By this time I also have a number of male friends, but our friendship is mainly comprised of kicking a football around. That's all the boys at school do—play football, or talk football.

I know that I'm a boy, biologically speaking. Due to being male, and also thanks in large part to my grandmother's fortnightly question, I feel strongly that I'm required to find females attractive. To fulfill this requirement, I randomly pick a girl from the class to be my first crush. As a boy, after all, I need to have a crush on a girl—otherwise others will think I'm too different

Age 12

My parents feel 12 is the age for me to learn about sex. It is a very distinct and somewhat scarring experience.

The year is 1996, and it is a fine Saturday morning. The sun blazes in the cloudy blue sky. Like every Saturday morning, rain or shine, me, my two brothers, and a friend from down the road are watching TV and playing with our Sega Master system. Routine is important.

Suddenly, my father calls us all to the kitchen. He's just finished chopping wood for the fire, and wants to talk to us.

We don't go right away, though—my brother Tommy, the eldest, is in the middle of completing a level of *Alex Kidd in Miracle World,* and we're all enthralled by the game. Alex Kidd is my favorite game character—he's way cooler than Mario or Sonic. So what, Sonic? All you do is go fast. So what, Mario? You like plumbing and pizza, and we never get pizza in our house. But Alex is someone I can identify with—he's just a normal kid, like me.

After a few moments of waiting, my father calls us again. "Come on, before it's too late," he warns.

My brothers and I hurry into the kitchen. Stephen, our friend from down the road, doesn't join us because he's in the bathroom.

"Okay, finally you're all here," my father says. "Guess what? Today you're learning about sex. I'm not going to go through this twice, so you're in whether you like it or not." He points out the window, where our family cat Dipper is humping

Patches, the cat from next door. "Look out the window," he says. "That is how you have sex."

This evokes different reactions from each of us.

Tommy says, "Way to go, Dipper. Good on you! Get that other cat!"

Chris, the middle child, goes, "Right, I've really got to get this down. Bite the girl on back of her neck and ear, and make sure she squeals."

While Tommy and Chris laugh, Stephen returns from the bathroom. He's younger than me, but started school early so he's a year ahead of me. He walks into the kitchen, looks out the window, and says, "Look, those two cats are doing it. Neat, do you all see it?"

I am quietly horrified by all of this. I want to say, "No, Dipper, get off Patches," but I keep this to myself.

court of law. Where has the time gone?

Some of my friends now have girlfriends. One girl in our class actually dropped out of school four years earlier after getting pregnant, although we only talk about this in hushed tones—never higher than whispers. It might not even be true.

Despite my father's lesson six years earlier, the subject of "sex" still doesn't really grab my attention. When someone mentions the general sexiness of a celebrity, I usually drift off. I only wake back up when the conversation gets to something that interests me. It rarely does.

Being young and wanting to fit in, I attend my high school graduation. This ceremony is where we say goodbye to our innocence and become adults. We've been waiting for this for 18 years. But I have to wonder why exactly we were waiting for this. Has anything really changed?

After graduation, we all go to the pub, and then on to a nightclub. As always, my first priority is fitting in, so I start drinking. At some point, I feel a tap on my shoulder. It's Rebecca, my childhood friend. I lost touch with her when I was 13, despite her only living a mile away from me, because we were sent to different high schools. She's changed so much since then—she's a grown woman now—whereas I feel like the same person I've always been.

Rebecca says hi, and then introduces me to her friend, Beth. She calls me her "ex-boyfriend." I never knew that we were going out. When did it start? When did it end? I had thought we were just friends that got on really well. There was nothing physical between us, and I had never wanted there to be—I thought of Rebecca only as a friend.

I think her misunderstanding was due to the fact that we were friends of opposite sexes. At that time, girls and boys didn't hang out unless they were dating. I had thought it was just an unconventional friendship, but for Rebecca, it was obviously something more.

Age 21

It's my final year of college, and I'm doing an exam on an accountancy computer program. I have to go through the transaction list, save it to a floppy disc, and hand it in. But at the end of the exam, I can't eject the floppy disc. My lecturer, Mr. Quinn, has to come over and remove it for me.

Later, I'm approached by a fellow student named David, from the town of Muff. A lot of people find

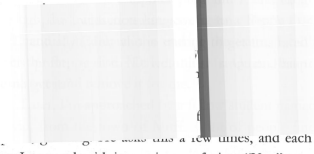

... asks this a few times, and each time I respond, with increasing confusion, "Yes."

Eventually Edel, who is starting to get frustrated at this point, says to David, "Just stop it. Philip doesn't get it."

Age 24

One of the scariest things that can happen to a man has happened to me—I've found a lump on my testicle. It's painful and sore. I notice it on a Thursday before a bank holiday weekend, so I have to wait four days before I can see my doctor the following Tuesday. The stress that the waiting causes me is indescribable.

On Tuesday afternoon, I finally see my doctor. He asks me to take off my trousers and underwear and get on the table to be examined. Then he puts on plastic gloves and feels the lump on my testicle. I prepare myself for the worst.

But he doesn't tell me what's wrong. He just relaxes, and says, "You can get up now and put back on your trousers." He returns to his desk while I put my clothes back on, and adds, "Come back to me in a month and I'll re-examine you."

I'm dying here. He won't tell me what's wrong, and he wants me to wait another month to find out? I'd thought five days was a long wait! "Why do I have to wait a month?" I ask.

"To see if it clears up," he says.

I'm starting to think I should ask to see his medical practitioner's license when he finally tells me what's going on. "It's blocked up sperm. It might clear up on its own, but it may not."

"Why did it happen?" I ask.

"The usual cause is lack of masturbation and sex," he says.

"Oh," I say quietly. I think back to conversations my friends had about masturbation, ones where I always stayed quiet because I knew my friends would look at me like I had two heads if I told them I had no interest in masturbating. Keeping my mouth shut was much easier than being honest about something I knew they'd never accept.

The only person I tell about the lump besides my doctor is my friend Jack. He asks me if it's an STD. "Nah," I say. "I think it's more like an anti-STD."

Age 27

My friends are getting married and having children, but I'm not. I look at them and think, "What are they

...y getting invited to stag nights and stag weekends. During my old friend Stephen's stag weekend, we go to a nightclub. Three of us guys are on the dancefloor—I move my arms and feet in an attempt at dancing, although sober onlookers are probably wondering if I'm having a seizure.

A girl approaches me and starts grinding on me to get my attention. I feel really uncomfortable, and try to ignore her.

The following night, one of the guys who was with me on the dance floor—Mike—is telling the story to the others in our group. "The hottest girl in the place was just grinding on Philip, but he was having none of it."

He repeats this story three times, obviously hoping for an amused reaction. But all he gets are knowing smiles. That's because he's told Stephen and my two friends Jack and Ben, and I came out to all three of them as asexual six months earlier. They know exactly why I was "having none of it."

In total, I've come out to six of my friends so far. They've all accepted it, and their responses are all along the lines of, "As long as you're the same person you've always been, you're still our friend."

I can't tell you how relieved I am by this response. I've spent my whole life hiding behind a mask. But now I'm out to my closest friends, and they didn't change their view of me when they found out about my asexuality. It feels so good to know they're finally seeing the real me. They like me for who I am, and that's all I've ever wanted. They are real friends.

Coming Out
Melissa Keller

Melissa Keller has been an avid writer since her childhood, and has written extensively on queer issues—both in her personal life, and through literature and academia. Aside from writing, Melissa enjoys studying history and social justice, acting, and traveling.

My high-school Anthropology teacher once asked us to write a list of the traits and characteristics we looked for in a sexual partner. I had no idea what to write, and was immediately put off by his assumption

points another way. I moved on with my life.

A few years later, in college, my final project for an English class was an essay concerning my experiences with sexuality and sexual relationships. Once again, I found myself explaining to my professor that I was asexual, and why that was pertinent to our topic: Women's Literature. Similar to the reaction of my high-school teacher, she asked a few questions, but eventually permitted me to write on that topic. I moved on with my life.

To this day, I am only "out" to two adults: those professors. Although both were influential in their teaching styles and subject matter, neither is one I would call a dear friend or mentor. Coming out was simply a necessity in order to get a grade. I thought nothing of it at the time, and it was not some momentous occasion greeted with a cake and streamers.

For many in the queer community, coming out is a rite of passage. I use the term "queer" as an overarching label for all those who do not identify as heteroromantic, heterosexual, and cisgender. For us, coming out is the time when you finally let yourself be truly open to family and friends, either accepting the love they share or dealing with the fallout.

There are internet forums, books, and even web series dedicated to the struggles of coming out. They provide tools and motivation to help young queer kids accept themselves, with or without the approval of their loved ones. We hear motivational stories from people like Ellen DeGeneres, Neil Patrick Harris, and Elton John about finally overcoming their fears of being—specifically—gay.

But for asexual people, there's rarely cheering when we come out. Sure, there can be love and acceptance, but a lot of the time there's confusion, irritation, and sometimes even hate. And for me, I consistently find, there's just no incentive to come out.

My thought process concerning coming out has always centered around telling my parents. Who better to accept me the way I am than the people who raised me? But I haven't come out to them, and I never plan to. Friends will ask if my parents are homophobic or bigoted, and the answer is no. I have no doubt they would accept me any way I am. The real question is: Why would they care that I'm asexual?

I imagine that if I bring home a girl, they might ask if I'm

differences between romantic and sexual identities, which would no doubt confuse my parents even further. This distinction proves to be complex even to some who identify themselves as queer.

As for my sexual preferences, what does it matter to them who I have sex with? I've never been comfortable discussing sex of any kind with my parents, so why start now?

But coming out is not just about sex. There is a wide consensus, among both queer and straight people, that if you don't come out, you're not comfortable with your identity. Self-hate, internalized homophobia, and so on. But let me tell you that I am very comfortable with my sexuality. In fact, I consider it one of my defining characteristics. Being asexual is very much a part of my identity, and I would never consider it an embarrassment or a flaw. I love who I am, and being "out" has nothing to do with that.

A large number of asexual people have had rough experiences in coming out. A cisgender, white guy coming out as gay may create feelings of relief and understanding, but when asexual people come out, we're often met with disdain, confusion, and sympathy.

"You're just a late bloomer."

"Are you sure?"

"That's not a real identity."

"You're not a plant! You can't be asexual."

"Who hurt you to make you feel this way?"

This is intertwined with the sense of "otherness" those who identify as asexual feel in both queer and straight communities alike. We can't flaunt our sexuality as would a gay or bi person. Walking down the street holding hands with someone will not be cause for controversy. There's no real way to show asexuality other than by saying: "Hey, I'm asexual." Our invisibility makes it difficult for us to participate in queer communities. After all, you can't identify as something that doesn't exist, and many people are convinced asexuality doesn't exist.

For something that is so intrinsic to the queer identity—coming out—the thought of it has never given me the euphoric feeling of openness that others in the queer community experience. It just feels uncomfortable. Unnecessary. Regardless, I am happy with who I am. I am comfortable with my identity and the life it affords me. My choice to keep my identity private is not a sign of weakness. It is proof

Being "Normal" Is Overrated Anyway

Ren

Ren is an 18-year-old from a small town in Pennsylvania. She loves animals, music, and art. This is her first published story.

Asexuality and I have had a rocky relationship. Although I've only recently learned the word, I've been battling with being asexual for my entire 17 years of living.

Since I was a little girl, I've been told how my life will turn out. "Someday you'll start feeling different about boys." "When you get married, you'll act like that, too." "Now, I know you're going to start wanting to have sex, but you need to use protection." I've always had trouble believing these things, but adults know better, right? They've lived longer, so they must know what they're saying.

As I grew up, I took pride in being able to prove these statements wrong. I thought I was being good and mature by not fawning over boys, or changing my appearance so guys would want to date me, or sneaking into the slide to make out with Tommy during recess. As I watched my friends go crazy over boys, I quietly thought to myself that I must have better self-control than them. Why else would they be acting the way they were?

In first grade, my best friend told me he liked me, and I didn't talk to him for a year. For some reason, that just seemed like what I was supposed to do. I think that at the time I thought I wasn't allowed to be dating anyone. As the years passed, boys told me they liked me, or even tried to kiss me. But I always turned them down. I had a few pursuers, but I was also a bit of a nerd, so people got over the fact that I didn't like them back pretty quickly.

I mostly managed to avoid boys all the way up to eighth grade (either by acting like a boy, or by not speaking to boys at all). It was in this year, though,

He and I would walk to and from class together, seeing as we were going to the same places, and we would joke and chat with the other kids going in the same direction. However, as the year went on, he started to pay more and more attention to me. I'll admit it was flattering, but it also set off a few red flags. So I decided to do to him what I'd done with every boy who had ever liked me before—ignore him until he went away.

Except he didn't go away. After six months of refusing to speak a word to him, he still talked to me every day. He'd thrown a wrench into my grand plan and ruined it. So, now what? At that point, I decided that if he could stick with me for that long without me saying a word to him, he must be worth something. So I started talking to him again.

For the next year, we were practically inseparable. I knew he wanted to date me, but there was a part of me that knew I shouldn't. I convinced him to date another girl, thinking that it would make him realize he didn't want to date me. Their relationship didn't last long, and by the end of it, I just felt bad. He had liked me for years, and I felt nothing for him—so much so that I'd pushed him into a relationship he didn't want. I felt so bad, in fact, that I convinced myself I had to have some feelings for him—it only made sense, considering how strong his feelings were for me. That was how it worked, right? I'd grow into it, for sure. So, by sophomore year of high school, I finally caved and said I would date him.

It wasn't bad, I guess. It just meant hanging out more and telling people we were dating. Eventually he did kiss me, breaking my age-old rule of having too much self-control to go around kissing boys. But then, you're supposed to kiss the person you're dating, right? So why not try it myself?

Kissing wasn't repulsive, but it also wasn't exciting like I read about in novels. I started to think I was doing something wrong, because it didn't feel like much of anything. Apparently he didn't think I was doing it wrong, because he started wanting more than that. He would ask me if we could have sex, or do this or do that, and I knew it wasn't even an option, but I never quite knew why. After a few months of me refusing, our relationship went sour and he broke it off. In retrospect, it was probably because of the lack of sex, but that didn't make sense to me at the time.

After that fiasco, I had a lot to think about. I had

discovered between my now-ex-boyfriend and I on subjects related to sex, I started to wonder whether I really was "in the norm."

I spent many nights sitting up in my bed, having conversations with myself as I tried to figure out what could be going on with me. Was I gay? I mean, I didn't want to have sex with boys, so that meant I had to want sex with girls by default. Right? But that didn't feel right either. I also did a lot of Googling and reading and watching of online content about what could be wrong with me. Finally, I came upon the term "asexuality."

That one took a lot more thinking. Asexuality made sense, and fit my "symptoms," but I couldn't be different, could I? What would my parents say when I told them they'd never get grandchildren from me? How would my friends feel if they knew I was on the wrong side of sexuality? Would they even believe me?

It was hard, and terrifying, to think that everything I had ever believed about my own sexuality could be false. My whole life was based off the few things I knew for sure about myself, and now one of those things was being flipped on its head. It took a lot of soul-searching, and a few nights of crying, for me to be able to accept that I might be different than I had thought. But eventually I was honest with myself, and I could finally say that yes, I really am asexual, and no matter what anyone else thinks or feels, that is the truth.

Due to the nature of modern society, I spent years pushing the truth away and refusing a part of who I am because I never realized asexuality was even an option. Thankfully, though, asexuality has never given up on me. It's stuck with me all these years, always in the back of my mind, helping to guide me through life. And the best part? It's never going to try to seduce me into its bed.

Finding Grace (The Gray-Ace Sex Life of a Gen X-er)

Betty Badinbed

Betty Badinbed is a Kiwi who's been resident in Australia since the turn of the century. She writes advertising copy for a living, reads obsessively, is a complete Tolkien nerd, and loves to travel—during which she collects anecdotes, hotel shower caps, and airline sick bags.

"There's no two ways about it," my friend Bryan states. "Everyone needs sex."

"Is that a fact?" I reply, in a dryly amused tone.

"Of course. It's a given fact of life. That's what it is to be human."

Bryan is theorizing based on the behavior of people he knows, and recent happenings.

"Surely not everyone," I venture, because I know otherwise. "What about nuns and monks and stuff?"

"Nope, you're wrong. Everyone needs sex. It's the underlying motive of all our behavior and social comings and goings. Nuns and monks have chosen to be celibate, so they've shut down that side of themselves. Deep inside, though, they need it too."

I decide not to disagree, because I don't want to say anything controversial. I'm not ready to explain myself—or worse, defend myself—against accusations of personal confusion. But what I want to say is this: not everyone needs sex, and I know because I'm one of those people. Though sex has definitely featured in my life as I strive to find my footing.

* * *

For a good 20-plus years of my adulthood, I had no idea asexuality was a thing. I did, however, think I was sexually dysfunctional, and that there was some sort of disconnect between my brain and my body. That really affected my self-esteem through my 20s and 30s. I was different; I seemed to have no sense of sexual self.

I was the only girl in my year group who never had a boyfriend during high school. While I did

"drive" to make things happen. I had no idea how to flirt, or read and send sexual signals. It just didn't come naturally. I seemed to "friend zone" people without even trying.

Despite all this, I continued to move with the great tide of humanity surrounding me, searching for that perfect someone with whom I'd have romantic times and great sex. Because that's just what people did.

* * *

In an unusual moment of bravery and desperation, with encouragement from a friend, I ring up a guy I fancy and ask him out. We go for a Mexican meal—me at my brightest and quirkiest, he aloof at first but gradually becoming more animated. At the end of the evening, we are standing by his front door. I don't know what will happen now, and he has both hands in his pockets. He is smiling, though. A shock of black hair hangs gorgeously over his blue eyes.

"Thank you for this evening," I say.

"No, thank you," he replies.

"Don't get me wrong," I continue. "I just want to be friends …"

Idiot. What a way to confuse someone. You don't ask a guy out to dinner and then tell him you want to be "just friends." The words blurted thoughtlessly from my lips, as though my psyche was trying to protect me from danger. I want to slap myself.

Not surprisingly, that was the end of that relationship.

* * *

A guy who I befriend in my late 20s tells me he used to see me at university years ago. In fact, he'd had his eye on me.

"Why didn't you ever say hello?" I ask.

"I was shy," he replies. "And my mate said 'don't bother with that one, you won't get anything from her.' We used to call you the Ice Queen—you didn't respond to the little attentions we sent your way. You were oblivious to us."

I am floored; I had no idea. I'm simply not aware of the looks people give each other, sizing up potential partners, flirting, or, at the very least, noticing.

* * *

My friends, in my 20s, were quite promiscuous. We'd go out to our favorite nightclub where they'd "pick up"—pursuing hot sex, or love, or simply the fun of seeing a drunken flirtation to its conclusion—while I inevitably went home alone. But I was never considered unusual by my loving, inclusive friends. They would simply note that their

up at our club. A sweet young guy has latched onto me. He's like glue; I simply can't shake him off. I am even mildly rude to him, but it's like water off a duck's back. The flattery from being adored kicks in, and I let him walk me home. But at the gate I finally manage to reject him, saying, "I'm sorry, I just don't want to."

I enter the house alone, thankful that I have managed to shut the whole thing down before reaching the bedroom. Once there, it's so much harder to call things off. To show disinterest between the sheets is to risk being called "frigid," a term that implies coldness. Cold I am not—too sensitive is what I am.

* * *

What I was looking for was love, as were all my friends. They attempted to find this in one-night stands. I watched people move together and come apart. I listened to my friends compare notes on contraception and STD clinics, and trade "regretting it in the morning" anecdotes. I watched them slink off to have abortions. I felt shy and awkward, having had only two partners at that stage while my friends shagged their way into double figures. I felt like I was just an observer, not fully participating in life.

Silly, foolish me. I was, without realizing it, just carefully looking out for myself.

* * *

It's a big party, and Bevan and I are flirting at last, now that he's single. Or rather, he flirts and I practice responding, pleased at no longer being my usual wallflower self, hoping my friends are taking note. I recall Mags, one of Bevan's exes, saying what a fantastic lover he was—very sexy, with a great technique in bed. I wonder if Bevan could break the spell over me. Could he unlock my dormant passion, find my G-spot, initiate me into the great secret of sex that has everyone enthralled but me?

When the proposition comes, I decide to risk a rare one-night stand, even though I don't feel "the hots" for him. Yet, I hope. I have his technique to look forward to. He's going to "cure me."

The technique, it turns out, is for Bevan to flutter his tongue in and out rapidly as he passes it across my body. I am both disgusted and amused—so this is the great lover! It's all I can do not to laugh out loud. Eventually I have to ask him to stop, apologetically claiming alcohol-related tiredness.

Bevan is very civil in the morning as he makes me tea and toast, while I chat politely with his housemates. The great lover's method has failed; he looks deflated. Yet, if he has silently branded me "frigid" or a closeted lesbian, he keeps it to himself. At least, no gossip reaches my ears.

like it might work out, because he didn't have the greatest libido, which suited me fine. It should have lasted longer, but had a geographical ending when he moved cities for work.

The partnerships in my 20s would generally end after three months or so. The boyfriend would lose interest because the sex wasn't great, and their "honeymoon period" attraction had worn off. I understand that now, but back then I thought the reason for my failed relationships could only be because I was unlovable.

All of this was taking place well before the internet. In my early 20s, I had read an entry in some stupid, misguided psychology/biology book about people who have a piece of their brain missing. It said that those people tended to be highly sensitive, prone to anxiety, and generally not attracted to either sex. Why, *I* was sensitive and prone to anxiety! Did that mean I was missing part of my brain?

This idea obviously filled me with horror. I'd been kind of hoping I was gay, and skirting nervously around the edge of that without doing anything about it. But after reading that book, I put off experimenting with a woman. I wanted to delay the inevitable truth: that, if I had as little luck with women as with men, I must be one of these "missing a piece of my brain" people the book mentioned.

Despite operating in the "mainstream straight world," though, I never felt part of it. For some time I had been informing myself about the gay lifestyle and queer issues, and supporting pride marches. Then, in my early 30s, through a new friendship, I started hanging out with a large group of gay men and women and going to clubs and bars with them. I was shy of the women. Lesbians seemed a world apart; my bi-curiousness shrank before their confidence and self-assuredness. I was sure I had a big neon sign over my head proclaiming my naivety.

But being with my male gay friends was fun. Sometimes I would be the only woman accompanying a large group of guys going out, and I was always looked after. "You'll never find yourself a man if you're always hanging with gay boys," straight friends would caution me. But I felt I'd found my place. Male company and close friendship without the sexual tension. Ideal.

It was around this time that I discovered taking recreational ecstasy felt pretty darn good, and also let

was making love to, not my bed partner.

* * *

I'm at a night club with my gay buddies, dressed for the occasion in a sexy, sheer black top that suits me well. I've been dancing freely for some time and take a break at the bar, where a man approaches me. He and his wife have been watching me, he says, and they'd like me to join them for their first ever "ménage à trois" at their place. He seems very nice, not at all sleazy. Would I despise myself if I turn down the kind of naughty encounter that "normal" people love to have? Perhaps this is the kinky moment that will unlock me! But no ... I will let everyone down. I can't accept his proposal.

Then the euphoria of a second pill starts to hit on my brain, and I say, "Nice to meet you, Jon. Lead the way."

Jon and I are on a mattress on the floor, while Suzy lounges on the sofa.

"Make her scream, Jon," she pants.

I am suddenly embarrassed. "Um, that's not going to happen," I mutter, pleading drug impotency. Then I am invited to go down on Suzy. She lies down, passive. It's her first time, too, and I don't know what to do. I make a few stilted moves, feeling like an actor in a play who hasn't learnt the lines. Soon, with embarrassment, I excuse myself and say I'd rather watch them. And I do watch, fascinated, as I might watch a nature documentary. I don't feel turned on, but I do feel privileged to witness this moment of intimacy between two people who love each other.

The best part of the whole encounter comes the next day, when I call my gay bestie and proclaim that I'd gone off for a threesome the night before.

"Oh you naughty, naughty minx!" he shrieks with delight. I am pleased. I've had a kinky sexual adventure I can now use as an anecdote.

* * *

In 2004, I went to see the film *Kinsey*. Afterwards, I curiously looked up the Kinsey Scale online. Exploring the links around that, I saw the word "asexuality," and within a few clicks I'd found AVEN. I was so amazed, stunned, and relieved by the articles and posts that tears started streaming down my cheeks. I read and learned avidly, and acceptance of myself began.

But it wasn't easy. I didn't embrace my new understanding with open arms, and at times felt very upset about it. I needed to talk to someone. Surely, if there were thousands of people on AVEN, there must be someone that I could talk to about it together. I thought I might try a psychiatrist who was someone with medical

"Inappropriately touched then? You may have suppressed the memory."

She continued to probe. I told her about AVEN and asked her to familiarize herself with it before our next appointment. When that time came, she hadn't. That was my last appointment with her.

* * *

My gay friend and I are both a little drunk, and I am morose. I have been "stood up" by a date that day and, dwelling on how hard it is to find someone, I burst into tears.

"I'm asexual," I blub to my friend. It's my first revelation to someone I know.

I expect he of all people will understand. But his response astonishes me. He grabs me by the shoulders and all but shakes me. "Don't you ever say that about yourself!" he shouts.

I am gob-smacked and try to explain, try to tell him about AVEN, but he won't listen, and I am too much of a stunned mess to push the point. Then he tells all our mutual friends about my confession. I receive a message of concern from one of them. "You're a lovely person," she writes, "you don't need to be so down on yourself."

It is 2005, and it seems awareness of asexuality is zilch. This is my chance to stand up, be proud, explain. But I am weak and unsure. I take it underground and don't bring it up again. In any case, my cause was not helped by my entering into a relationship with the guy who stood me up. (Turns out he was in the hospital suffering from a venomous spider bite!)

Our relationship goes on to last nine happy years.

* * *

No matter the nature of our sexuality—or lack thereof—our lives are full of difficulties, little and large. I look back on my difficulties and note how they are balanced by wonderful friendships. And I think about all the positive things being asexual has brought to my life.

First, the independence. I developed this from a realization that I may be living alone for large chunks of my life, if not all of it. (As I'm writing this, I have yet to actually live with a partner.) My youthful uncertainty has been replaced by a sense of freedom and self-preservation.

Second, I managed to escape the massive relationship dramas, the jealous lovers, the stalkers, the abortions, and the unhappy "too young" marriages that have plagued several of my friends. Retaining a sort of innocence and youthful vigor, I look 10 years younger than I am, and I will hopefully [illegible]

[illegible] and other things that are "better than sex." Like any good geek who isn't chasing a libido, I've devoted much time and love to these things.

Now, what about the relationships I've had over the years? They include:

The deep, platonic friendships with straight guys. My friend-zone barriers have allowed for some amazing long term friendships to develop. Once guys recognize that I'm not going to hit on them or cause complications in the area occupied by their girlfriends, I am treated as a confidante—"one of the guys," a buddy, a sister.

There was the impotent boyfriend I had for a while. He was suffering from self-esteem issues that were threatening to keep him celibate. He found in me someone who didn't care about his problem (and who was secretly relieved by it), and we had fun while both finding a time-out from our issues.

Following that was a three year relationship in which my boyfriend called off "the sex bit" after just three months. He wouldn't explain his reasons. But we went on to have a very fulfilling platonic relationship for the rest of our time together. It didn't seem to need a label or an explanation, it just "was."

And then there's the aforementioned nine year relationship with a sexual guy. I never confided my status to him; I simply told him I had "the world's lowest libido." And he was very understanding and patient; he never held it against me, never got stroppy about his needs for gratification. Yes, these men do exist. And because of this, and his very loving and affectionate nature, I tried harder, and was able to satisfy him sexually from time to time. His pleasure was my pleasure.

I'm now in my late 40s, and I seem to have developed a small injection of "mojo," bringing the gray areas of my asexuality to the forefront. I'm now reading erotica and watching sexy films. I see attractive people on the street and acknowledge them to myself with joy. A gorgeous smile, nice eyes, the ability to wear their clothes well. It doesn't need to go any further than this acknowledgement; I don't experience any frustrated libido.

There's a recently-coined term for a behavior that I now realize is a part of myself: autochorissexuality. This is essentially a disconnect between a person and a sexual target or object. I might get aroused by sexual fantasies, or to erotica or [illegible]

[illegible] parties, and I dream of a day when asexuals can create enough critical mass and confidence to hold a massive pride party of their own. No matter where it is in the world, I would be there.

* * *

As I write this, I am fending off the text message advances of an acquaintance—already partnered— who wants to have an affair with me. In my much younger days of uncertainty, the flattery that "someone wanted me" may have caused me to proceed, with scruples over the "cheating" aspect being the main bother. But now, though I kind of like him, I am firm in my resolve. I will save us the mutual embarrassment, I will not interfere with an existing relationship, and ultimately, I don't need sex.

Unlike what Bryan thinks.

Black Women
Can Be Asexual Too
Gabriella Grange

Gabriella Grange is a 21-year-old African-American demiromantic asexual who hails from Texas. She is a rising senior at Smith College who is also a philosophy major and an Afro-American Studies minor. She loves her Nichiren Buddhist practice, tea, books, knitting, cello, and, of course, discussions about asexuality.

I'm an asexual woman who also happens to be black.

because I was worried about what people would think (I'm a native Texan). This gave guys the excuse to hit on me, although I never returned their interest. I also joined my school's Gay-Straight Alliance—in retrospect I realize that, as a sexual minority, I empathized with those adolescents in the LGBTQ community.

Throughout high school, I thought my lack of interest in dating or sexual activity was because my parents wanted me to focus on my studies and cello performance. But then I got to college and away from my parents, and I still wasn't interested in dating or sex. I even had a chance to explore my bisexuality, thanks to my school being a historically all-women's college with a sizeable LGBTQ population. But I soon discovered I was uninterested in dating or having sex with either men or women.

I became confused for quite some time. Was I not bi anymore? If not, what on Earth was I? How could I identify as bisexual (or any default orientation, for that matter) when I never talked or thought about anything related to sex?

Before my first year of college, I attended a summer program and met my first asexual person. She told me that kids at her school made fun of her for being asexual. I empathized with her, and told her how every time guys would hit on me I would reject their advances. She suggested I might be aromantic.

Then, in the second semester of my first year, I took a music workshop and met a beautiful participant who took me back to her room so we could chat. I noticed she had the asexual flag on her wall, so I asked her about it, and she told me about it and about how she was demisexual. But I still didn't identify as asexual at the time; I still thought I was bi.

In my sophomore year of college, I took a summer course at Hampshire College in Amherst, Massachusetts. I was nervous about meeting new people, since I'm rather shy and introverted. Then, on the second day of the course, I was working with this guy my age that was also shy and introverted. At first I was indifferent to him, but then he told me about how he spent three years going to school in Uganda, and I became aesthetically attracted to him. I also wanted to be his friend and hang out with him because I thought he was awesome.

We lost touch after the program because I didn't have Facebook and that was the only way he communicated. But a few months later, I saw him and

we even hugged, which seemed to surprise her—she probably thought I would be frosty toward her, or that we would become instant rivals, or something.

After this meeting, I questioned my feelings. If I didn't want to date this guy, why couldn't I stop thinking about him? Then I found AVEN over winter vacation, and everything began to click. I realized that I didn't experience sexual desire—I've never looked at someone and thought, "I'd have sex with them." I look at people and just think, "Oh, cool, a bunch of human beings, great."

When I found the asexual label for myself, I was hesitant about identifying as asexual because I didn't find many other black asexuals on AVEN. But then I read an article about a student at Temple University who just happened to have the same identities as me: a black female asexual! I also found a YouTube video of another African-American asexual girl who ran a blog called *Queer as Cat,* and another black asexual female blog called *Gradient Lair.* When I found these, I was happy and relieved. I thought, "Thank goodness I'm not the only one who is black, female, and asexual."

Once I realized I was asexual, I had to figure out my romantic orientation. For a while I thought I was aromantic, as the girl I met at summer camp suggested. In fact, I spent my entire junior year of college trying to figure out whether I felt romantic or platonic attraction toward people, and it frustrated me deeply. However, I've recently realized that I'm demiromantic, meaning I do not experience romantic attraction until I form an emotional connection with someone. And I discovered this because, for the first time in my life, I've found someone I feel a romantic attraction to.

I first met him at an orchestra rehearsal in my freshman year of college. He was a handsome, sweet, quiet young man, and after rehearsal he asked me for my number. We never went out, but it never bothered me because I was too busy with schoolwork to think about guys. Although we attend different colleges, we both study philosophy and take cello lessons from the same instructor. Even though we don't see each other often, we are always happy to see each other when we do meet up. At first I didn't feel any sexual or romantic attraction toward him, but after three years of seeing him perform beautiful cello solos with the utmost passion, and getting acquainted with his sweet, kind personality, I have realized he is the one.

I wanted *his* number. So he gave me his number, and we said our farewells. Since then, I haven't been able to stop daydreaming about dating, kissing, marrying, and raising children with this guy. I am happy to have finally found my romantic orientation, but even happier to have found him.

Being a black asexual has been an interesting experience so far. Although I have yet to meet another black asexual in person, I'm hopeful that as the asexuality movement progresses and the discourse on race and sexuality comes to include black asexuals, I might meet one when I least expect it.

So, thank you AVEN, thank you David Jay, Julie Decker, and all the other ace people out there. You guys rock my world.

Fixing What Isn't Broken

Emma Hopwood

Emma Hopwood is a 17-year-old American student dedicated to agricultural sciences and literature. She raises awareness for the queer community through videos, writing, and art.

Welcome! Welcome to planet Earth!

Welcome to the home of countless species, including the beautiful, amazing, stupendous human race!

Now, if you look to your right, you'll see a wild

... it's not about the love, is it? It's. All. About. Sex. Because the meaning of life is reproduction. There's an unwritten agreement that if you exist, you must pass on your genes. If not ... well, here's some news for you. You are a freak.

Well, I suppose I should introduce myself, then. You can call me an asexual. Quite simply, I don't want to do any of that sexual nonsense. Just cuddles and conversations over tea.

Not that I'm holding back at all.

If I had a choice, I would honestly rather go to my fridge and eat some cake rather than have someone stick their tongue down my throat.

And no, I am not a freak.

But ...

well

people think I am...

and sometimes so do I.

...

It was never an issue. Until one by one my friends were picked off by princes and women in white ... I smiled for them, but a part of me began to catch fire. It's not that I longed for a relationship—I was angry.

Angry enough to yell at my reflection. To ask her what made her broken, why she couldn't feel. Why she gave a damn in the first place.

Tentatively, I reached out to others with manic questions, begging for an explanation.

You need to try it first.

But that's the thing. The thought of it *bores* me. If you were asked to write a book on making a sandwich, would you want to? No? How do you know if you haven't tried?

Too young?

Look around. Just. Look. Around.

I can fix your problem ...

Back off.

It's no surprise that I felt broken, considering I was surrounded by horny teens, naked ladies on TV, and sex-saturated magazines.

And I know some of these things won't change. But awareness can. And perhaps if we teach people that *asexuality isn't fake ...*

... well, maybe they'll stop trying to fix what isn't

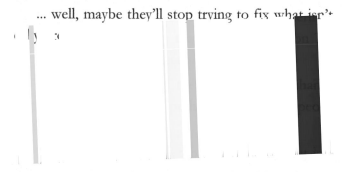

I Just Don't Get It

Jennifer Dyse

Jennifer Dyse is a 20-year-old freelance artist from Mississippi. She enjoys battling the forces of evil and helping NPCs with yard work. This is her first published story.

Hi. My name is Jennifer Dyse, and I am asexual.

When I was a little kid, my parents and my sister used to talk about their previous relationships a lot, and I never really understood their fascination with the topic. But I just shrugged off my confusion—when I'm older, I'll understand.

Around sixth grade, everybody was talking about who was hot and who was not. Once again, I didn't really get it. This made me start to think that maybe there was something wrong with me. But again, I just shrugged it off—when I'm older, I'll understand.

When I was in junior high I still didn't "get it," so I started faking it. I would see which guys everyone else liked and say I liked them too. That kind of backfired, though, because then my friends would tell me I should go ask those guys out, which I definitely didn't want to do. And sometimes those guys would come up to me, randomly, and ask me out. I never

67

knew what to do, so I just said no. This resulted in people thinking I was kind of weird.

By the time I reached high school I still had no interest in dating, so I decided to "fix" myself by getting into a relationship with whoever asked me. That turned out to be the worst two years of my life, because he was really abusive and made me do things I didn't want to do. And, ultimately, that made me feel even more broken.

In my first year of college, I randomly decided one night to Google my "symptoms." I was tired of feeling broken, and wanted answers. That's when I found AVEN and discovered asexuality—and the definition fit! I thought, "Oh, I'm not broken—I'm just asexual." Around the same time, I realized I was aromantic, which explained why I never had an

way.

Now that I'm older, my being asexual isn't something I really think about on a daily basis, unless it comes up in conversation. And if it does, I'll just say I'm asexual. Most people don't know what that means, but I kind of like explaining it to them.

I think I found out about my asexuality at a good place in my life, before it became really, really destructive—well, no more destructive than the abusive relationship, I guess. I'm pretty content with where I am, and I love being asexual. And I also love myself, now that I know I'm not broken.

An Asexual Teen

Kaya Brown

Kaya Brown is an aspiring author from New England with a passion for travel. She currently runs two blogs: one about her adventures, and one about her creative writing.

I first heard the term asexuality when I was 15 years old. Before that, I had been afraid something was wrong with me, because my friends had been making sexual jokes for years and I never understood either the jokes or why my friends were making them when they were so young. Asexuality seemed to offer an

more, because I didn't understand the appeal of sex. I knew people my age "did it," but *why?* The only reason for sex was to have children, right? It was truly a shock for me to learn that my fellow teens weren't having sex because they were trying to rebel—they were doing it because they *enjoyed* it.

At that point, I considered identifying as asexual. However, after seeing posts saying things like: "If you're still young, you might not want to identify as asexual because if you change later on then people will call you a liar," I was hesitant about committing to it. I decided to wait—because, after all, maybe I wasn't asexual? Maybe I was hetero, or bi, or something else, and I just didn't realize it yet because I was too young.

Instead of being who I knew I was, I chose to wait to identify my sexuality until I was absolutely sure. I didn't want to misrepresent asexuality. If I identified as such, and then changed and identified as something else later on, I worried it would give people I knew an excuse to say asexuality wasn't real. I didn't want to invalidate an entire sexual orientation for my friends just because I was confused!

So, another year went by, and I rediscovered the term for a third time when I was 17. I thought, "This really fits me, so I'm going to start using it. Even if I don't tell anyone." And so, after two years of hesitancy, I finally started identifying as asexual, about a month after my 17th birthday.

Even then I still felt wrong—not because I didn't think I was asexual, but because I'd heard so many times that young people should wait to identify as asexual because they might change. I had some problems with anxiety and self-doubt already, which didn't exactly help me in my decision.

Eventually, I decided to come out to two friends who are huge queer community supporters. It went over fairly well—almost too well, actually, as if they just accepted what I said but didn't actually believe me.

When I decided to come out to my Mom, I eased her into the subject. First, I showed her a picture of "ace pride," and explained to her the "cake is better than sex" joke. She responded with something like: "Anyone who says that hasn't had sex!" Undeterred, I continued my education efforts. I sat her down and explained in depth what asexuality meant. I even started writing articles about it, and read what I'd written to her. Finally, while discussing one such

being asexual. Most are, but some want to change. I am proud of my sexuality, and I wouldn't change it for anything.

The biggest problem with being asexual as a teen, for me, is the distrust. In the past, I'd never

72

understood why girls and boys couldn't have mixed sleepovers, because I didn't think sex was really as big a deal as everyone made it out to be. I couldn't wrap my head around the concept that a girl and a boy couldn't be left alone in a room with the door closed because they'd *do something*, even with other people in the house. All my friends agreed with the idea, though, so I just went along with it. But despite the fact that none of those rules apply to me, I'm still a teenager—and when you're a teenager, nobody trusts you. They don't trust you to know yourself well enough to identify as asexual (and mean it!), and they *definitely* don't trust you to be alone with the opposite sex, regardless of whether you're asexual or not.

If you can know you're heterosexual or homosexual by the time you're 13 or 14, why should any other sexuality be different? The answer is: it shouldn't. But even assuring myself of that fact didn't help me come to terms with being asexual any more quickly.

I've been told by some people that eventually I'll be interested in sex because it's "natural." But I hate that idea, because it makes me seem weird, as if I'm some kind of freak of nature for not wanting to have sex. But I'm not weird, I'm not a freak of nature, and neither is anyone else who is asexual.

In a society that over-sexualizes constantly, it can be difficult to come out as someone who doesn't experience sexual attraction—and even harder to come out as someone who is disgusted by the thought of having sex. For anyone doubting who they are, or what their sexual orientation is, I'd like to give you this piece of advice: you know yourself better than anyone else knows you, and don't let anyone tell you otherwise.

Dream Guy

Cionii

Cionii is a Southern U.S. college student. Ze investigates music around the world and the many environmental dangers to people's health.

You tell me that I'm beautiful,
with the sunlight on my hair
You say my gaze is enchanting,
but I don't care
As long as you understand what's going on
behind these eyes of mine

Oh, by now I thought you'd see
This appearance has little to do with me
It's just a container for what's inside

When you say something kind
Or know what's on my mind
That's what I like about us

When you know what I'm saying
Hoping, wishing, or praying
That's what I like about us

CIONII

I like how we can talk for hours
And never run out of things to say
My true self never cowers
At what you're going to say

When I …
Act a little crazy
Say one too many "maybe"s

I know you'll get impatient sometimes
But at the same time
My true self never quivers, never fears
No mask here

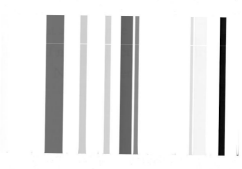

It's All Asexual To Me

Jarrah Shub

Jarrah is 15 years old and lives near Melbourne, Australia. She likes reading, mythology, and equality.

When I was young, everybody had a crush. All the other girls seemed to pick one boy and claim them. They would sit around, heads bent in secrecy, and everyone would give their reply to the question: "Who do *you* have a crush on?" I was never all that social with the other children, so I didn't get asked that question until several years into school.

When I was inevitably asked, I did pick a boy: Francis, who was shy and had unruly hair and pretty blue eyes. These were the main reasons for my selection of him—he was nice to look at, and I thought he might have an interesting personality.

Years later, after I moved schools, I was asked the same question at sleepovers. I deflected by saying that I once had a crush, Francis, at my old school. The knowledge that I used to have a crush was enough to prevent the girls from asking who my current crush was. It was a good thing they didn't, because I wouldn't have had an answer.

After a while, one of my friends started dating Francis. I was supportive and unaffected, if a little bored by her gushing about him all the time. I knew other girls would have reacted differently to the news of their old crush dating someone else, but it never bothered me that I didn't seem to feel the same way that other people did.

At some point, people tired of the crush question and moved on to actual dating. I thought I might be a lesbian, since I thought girls were nicer looking than boys, but I still didn't feel any attraction to them. I speculated that maybe my hormones just hadn't kicked in yet—although by that point I was well into my teen years, so that couldn't be the case.

Eventually I turned to the internet, and I struggled with the overload of new information. After

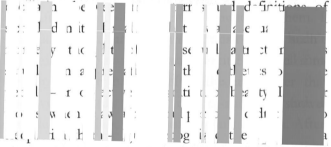

beautiful person.

Coming out to my parents wasn't really such a big deal. As far as I can remember, it consisted of me yelling down the stairs, "I'm asexual!" After that, there were a few lengthy conversations. I showed them the literature. My mother seems to think that one day I'll find "the one," we'll compromise, and I'll grudgingly have sex, at which point I'll realize I like it. My dad insists that asexuality is a made up word, and seriously doubts the whole thing. They still forget sometimes, and ask if there's anyone at school that I like, or if anyone likes me. They'll come around eventually. I hope.

The truth is I have a lot of trouble recognizing when someone has a crush on me. Apparently, boys still do that thing where they're mean or annoying to a girl they like. I thought we grew out of that when we grew out of our baby teeth. On my end, apparently some of the things I say can come across as flirting— but I just like interesting conversations and debates. It's not my fault if a boy reads too far into something because I'm smiling as I talk to him.

These days, I don't pretend to have crushes. If the topic comes up in conversation, I don't hide my asexuality. People might be surprised or even shocked, but they get over it. Maybe they just don't care because it doesn't seem real to them, or because it doesn't really impact their lives that much.

I do currently have a bet going with a girl that I will never have sex in my life. The prize is just pride and bragging rights. The plan is to meet up when we're really old so I can say, "I told you so." I think I might have sex one day, just to see what it's like, but at the moment even kissing seems gross to me.

At the moment, I still haven't figured out whether or not I'm aromantic. I know I don't feel any desire to be in a relationship or do romantic things. I'll never really know until I try it, I guess. I might even like all that hand-holding and hugging. Who knows?

I'm currently in my early teenage years, so sex really isn't all that prevalent in my life. People in my grade probably haven't gotten much past the kissing stage, despite their claims and all the gossip. Of the two couples I know, the first barely even speak to each other, and the other is always sickeningly affectionate. I'm sure that, as I get older, I'll be shoved headfirst into this sexual culture. But it will be

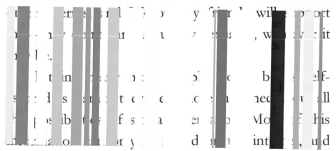

my peers are too busy with sports and socializing to venture as far as I have. If our culture was more accepting of change and differences, then we could be more educated and our identities could be more tailored to us, personally.

Right now, I'm happy with who I am, and I intend to continue along as usual—reading books, fast-forwarding through unnecessary sex scenes (because, come on, I'm sure that just this once you could solve the mystery without making out first), and being generally introverted. I still don't entirely understand the world, although that's nothing strange—nobody really does. But as long as I keep learning more about the world and about myself every day, I think that's something I can live with.

When I Grow Up

Shannon Brown

Shannon is a 17-year-old aspiring writer from the UK. She enjoys playing guitar, reading, and long walks on the beach. Planning on studying English and Creative Writing at university, she wants to write TV scripts in the future.

I had my first sexual education lesson when I was 10 years old.

First, our class sat down and watched a strange video on puberty. It started with a cartoon about a man and a woman falling in love, which for some

my teacher saying. "But make sure you're emotionally ready to have sex before you have it."

This is what I thought was wrong with me, growing up—I wasn't emotionally ready for sex. By the time I was 15 years old, people my age were having sex, or thinking about sex, and I ... well, I just wasn't interested. So, I assumed that I just wasn't ready—I was still too immature and childish to want sex.

When I reached 16, my friends started calling people "hot" and "sexy," but I was more interested in cuddling than anything else. Around this point in my life I joined Tumblr—and before you all groan, let me tell you that there is more help and information regarding sexuality and gender identity shared on Tumblr than in any school I've ever attended. On Tumblr, I found a post about asexuality in television characters. This was a term I had never come across before, so I Googled it and was astonished—I'd finally found a word that described me. Lots of people say labels are a bad thing, but when you think you're the only one feeling a certain way and you can fit a label to yourself, it means there are others like you. It means you're not alone.

As one might expect, not everybody understood my asexuality. Some of my friends, for example. While they accepted it on the surface, I could tell they didn't really get it. One friend told me that my opinions on people's attractiveness didn't matter anymore, which just isn't true—I may not feel sexually attracted to someone, but I can still tell if they're pretty or not, or if they're considered attractive by society.

The main issue some my friends had with my asexuality is that they didn't see why I felt the need to come out at all. It wasn't as if anything had changed since my coming out—I wasn't sleeping with people before, and I wasn't sleeping with people after. If it didn't affect my friends in any way, why was I even telling them?

I came out to my closest friend first (he's the one who told me I can't find people attractive), because I needed someone to know. I think I needed someone to explain asexuality to, to ensure that this word fit me and that I could use it. Having someone to talk to, so I could figure myself out, was incredibly helpful. The first time saying it was the hardest, but the more I said it, the easier it became.

Recently, I wrote a blog post about my

[several lines obscured]

grasp what asexuality is, and what it means to me.

For example, I tell them I view sex in the same way I view scuba-diving—it is something I am aware other people enjoy and love to do, but I don't really want to take part. However, if someone I loved asked me if I wanted to go, I might say yes, to make them feel good.

This is what lots of people (including a couple of people in my friendship group) don't understand— you can be asexual and still have/want/enjoy sex. It's different for every asexual person. And it causes a lot of discussion amongst my friends, but that's just how things are learned. You can't know something without being taught. Hence why I don't mind people asking questions.

I feel like which people you decide to come out to depends on the way your relationship works with them. I came out face to face with my closest friend, and then made a post on my blog which my other friends saw. I discovered that telling one person made it easier to tell others, and now I have no problem coming out to someone who doesn't know about my asexuality when the topic comes up.

A heads up, though, to anyone wondering if they're asexual—the entire world will try to tell you that you're not. I'm still worrying about whether or not I'm asexual even now, because it has been so ingrained into me that everyone will want to have sex at some point in their life.

The entire world doesn't know how you feel though, so don't listen to them. Listen to yourself. Sometimes, the entire world is stupid.

Just A Small Town Boy

Cameron

Cameron is a 20-year-old demi-heteroromantic asexual from Australia. He is currently studying a Bachelor of Agricultural Science at La Trobe University. Cameron's hobbies include indulging in copious amounts of alcohol and relaxing with his friends.

In order to understand my story, you first need to understand my backstory.

I grew up in a small town called Kyabram (Ky, as the locals call it). It's located in Victoria—a state in

a child.

Growing up, I spent most of my time on the farm, riding around on tractors, trucks, and motorbikes. I didn't really get into town except when necessary (haircuts, doctor appointments, etc.), and I didn't meet many kids my age until I started pre-school. But pre-school was only three days a week, so I remained pretty isolated. Because of that, I didn't have many friends when I started elementary school.

Given the size of the town, we kids weren't exposed to many different cultures or ideas that were considered outside the norm. And so the concept of sexuality wasn't introduced into the curriculum until about age 14/15. We only learned about the most common sexual orientations, like gay and straight. All the more obscure orientations slid under the radar, and the only way you found out about one of those is if you looked into it on your own. That's why I didn't know asexuality even existed until a few years ago.

My journey into asexuality started at age 17. I had been involved in a couple of relationships by that point, and was trying to become more involved with a friend who lived in Melbourne. We were talking on the phone when the conversation turned sexual, and we started describing sexual fantasies to each other. This was my first real experience with asexuality (that I can recall), because I found myself wondering why I wasn't aroused by any of the fantasies she described to me, no matter how vanilla or kinky they were.

A few weeks later, I got a call from the same girl. I think she realized I wasn't aroused by her sexual fantasies (which included me a lot of the time), and also that my own fantasies really had nothing to do with sex. She asked me whether or not sex appealed to me, and the immediate answer that came to me was, "No." I started my search for answers right after that.

With a quick Google search, I found myself on the front page of AVEN. Then I read through the FAQ. I still wasn't quite sure about my asexuality, so I made an account and went into the chatroom to ask a few questions. I was received warmly there, and had many things explained to me that made the picture a lot clearer.

Since that day, I have found myself an identity which makes sense to me and keeps me moving forward. I'm no longer stuck in this confused state of, "I like girls but I don't want to have sex with them. Maybe I'm gay? No, guys don't appeal to me at all. Then what am I?" It's a weight off my shoulders,

to help those in need to understand what's going on with them (or with their friend, or family member, or significant other).

To the person reading this: if you feel at war with yourself over what you think and feel and what you think you should be thinking and feeling, come to AVEN. You may discover things about yourself that you've never even thought of before.

Coming Out To Myself:
Not A Piece Of Cake

Ennis

Ennis is a 24-year-old artist from Massachusetts. She identifies as asexual-aromantic and demi-girl (or demi-female). Ennis paints in her spare time, focusing on historical events and figures that are often overlooked. She is passionate about art, history, and other cultures. She is always looking to educate others about asexuality and aromanticism.

I first realized I was asexual about two years ago. As a

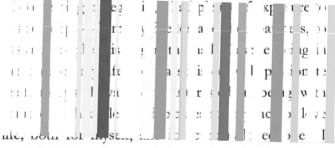

would think, "I'm too busy with my studies," or "There's no one at school who's my type," or "I'm too shy," or "I have Asperger's syndrome, so social interactions are too difficult."

I have had a grand total of two boyfriends in my life. The first one barely counts, so he only gets a passing mention. Introduced by a family friend, we were both too shy and awkward to really get anywhere. Six months and three dates later, I dumped him through a text message.

My second boyfriend and I had a proper relationship (sort of), and most of this story will involve him. We met at our university's commuter lounge. I was in my third year. We talked a lot in the lounge, and I soon realized we had a lot of common interests (history, music, etc.). I friended him on Facebook. We continued to spend time together at school, but then summer was on its way and the semester came to an end. We exchanged phone numbers over Facebook, and a month after classes ended he asked me out. I said yes. We lived half an hour away from one another, so our dates were limited by who had access to transportation.

He transferred to a different school after we started dating, so we didn't get to see each other often. Our work schedules clashed, so we mainly kept in contact with daily text messages. I found this non-physical relationship to be quite pleasant. I had made it clear when we started dating that I was inexperienced and largely uninterested in intimacy. I am an incredibly shy person, and I have Asperger's (or ASD), so I was always blaming these two things for my lack of interest in intimacy. I used my mental health as a shield to deflect any confusion I had about my sexuality.

My boyfriend agreed to take things slow. We had our first kiss on the third date. He took me to the movies and we saw the new Bourne movie. We held hands for most of the film, and I leaned into him during the intense scenes—typical date stuff. After the movie he asked if he could kiss me, and I said yes.

This was it, my first kiss! It was really happening! This had been built up in my mind as a beautiful moment, an amazing feeling. I was supposed to feel this burning passion surge through me. Society and cinema had planted this idea in my head—not to mention my peers gushing about their own experiences with their first kisses. I leaned in toward

health issues and my lack of experience. Surely I just needed more practice. Practice makes perfect, as they say. After all, my only previous experience with kissing was with a girl at camp, and even that was done just to be silly, to freak out an annoying but harmless homophobic girl. No intimate feelings were required.

As my relationship with my boyfriend continued, I started to doubt that my lack of experience or mental health was to blame for my disinterest in intimacy. Our conflicting schedules meant we rarely got to spend time together. The handful of times we could see each other were spent mostly talking or making out. I always got too uncomfortable when we tried to go any further than that, so we stuck to kissing. When our bodies touched, I kept waiting to get that burst of desire, to know with certainty that I wanted this, like I was supposed to. I tried to feel something, anything—that fierce passionate spark I always saw in movies. But, alas, there was nothing. Not even the dimmest ember.

As I said, we communicated primarily through texting. We would send each other text messages every day. "How are you?" "How's work/school?" "I miss you," etc. I could manage this type of relationship just fine. I generally prefer texting to talking on the phone anyway. This daily texting felt cute, like something a really young couple would do.

Sexting was a completely different story. I don't even know if what we were doing was considered sexting, or if we were just sending each other sexy texts. Remember, I had no previous experience with dating—I'd might as well have been trying to solve advanced calculus in Russian for all the luck I had understanding this. When he'd send me a flirty message asking what I'd do to him when I got my hands on him, I would often just stare blankly at my phone, unsure how to answer. I had no idea what I wanted to do to him—probably nothing as sexy as he was picturing. I never knew how to respond, but if there's anything growing up with Asperger's has taught me, it's that if you don't know how to act in a certain situation, you fake it. Learn what is socially expected of you in that situation, and do that. So that's what I did—I borrowed snippets of flirty, sexy talk I had picked up from pop culture, like some first year foreign language student awkwardly piecing together a comprehensible sentence.

Eventually, I decided to get over my intimacy

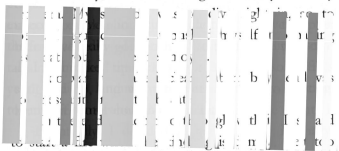

uncomfortable about the whole thing, so we stopped before we really got too far. We figured we would try again another time. We got back into out PJs, snuggled up, and went to sleep. I tried to shut my brain off, but I couldn't stop replaying the events in my head. Why was I so uncomfortable about sex? I'd had a very thorough sex education. Not one of those, "Don't have sex because you will get pregnant and die" experiences—it was actually very informative. If I wasn't squeamish about the subject on paper, why was I so freaked out about it in person? Was I just nervous? Are all women with Asperger's like this? Why don't I want to have sex with someone I love?

This was throwing me for a loop! Prior to that, I had felt like I had a pretty good understanding of who I was. I knew I was a woman (cis), and I knew I was an Aspie (Asperger's). I was happy about my appearance, and I didn't care if people had a problem with my body hair or lack of makeup. I had kind of assumed I was bi for most of my teen years (on the low end of the Kinsey scale), since I felt more or less the same toward boys and girls—i.e., indifferent. I'm sure if I'd known about non-binary genders before I knew I was asexual, I would have called myself "pansexual." I was content calling myself "bi," but not confident enough to come out. Despite my vaguely defined orientation, though, I was quite comfortable with myself—something that isn't often found in girls my age.

So, it was really scary to be suddenly confronted with not understanding something about myself. I knew I had to figure out what was going on with me, sexually, as soon as possible. I hated being confused about myself.

My boyfriend drove me home after the "sex" incident, and we spent most of the half hour trip in silence. Then my mom dropped me off at school, and that trip was also mostly silent. This "sexuality" issue was at the forefront of my mind, and it would not go away.

Because it never occurred to me to skip school so I could work out my identity crisis, I sat through a few hours of class before I could get to the library. It was a very interesting experience, trying to focus on quantitative reasoning and art history while at the same time panicking over my sexual orientation.

As soon as my last class let out, I rushed to a computer on the secluded third floor of the library. I

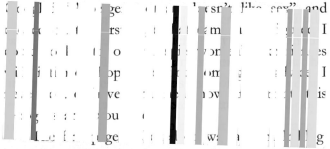

The blog explained that many women with Asperger's were also "asexual." It was the first place I had ever seen the word. There was no definition provided, but it was my first lead, like I was some TV detective on a case. I quickly typed the word "asexual" into Google, and AVEN was the first site to pop up. I didn't know what I was expecting to find when I clicked that link, but I am so happy I did. As I read AVEN's explanation of asexuality, it felt like a choir of angels singing to me. That's the best way I can describe the sense of relief I felt in that moment. I thought, "This is what I am! I'm not broken!"

It was one of the greatest moments of my life. I could almost forget I was in the university's library. I poured through AVEN's FAQs, and each piece of the puzzle slowly clicked into place. A great weight was suddenly off my chest, one that had been growing heavier in the past few months.

But my euphoria was brought crashing down to earth when I realized I would have to break up with my boyfriend. He had not signed on for a sexless relationship, and it would not be fair to expect him to agree to one.

I came out to my mom later that day. She was very supportive and proud that I had figured this out on my own.

I broke up with my boyfriend a week later. I'm not sure why I waited a week. Maybe I didn't want him to think the breakup was somehow his fault. Maybe I was avoiding the uncomfortable conversation. I knew our relationship was over, but I guess I just wanted to explain my feelings properly, and I couldn't have done that when I had only just figured out my sexual orientation a day ago. Knowing I shouldn't delay it any longer, I texted him that we needed to talk. He called me later that night, just as I was getting out of my anime club's weekly meeting. The breakup went quite smoothly, I think. I don't have much experience with breakups, but there were no tears, no yelling, and a mutual agreement that we should go back to being just friends (we didn't, but that's unimportant). I had to explain what asexuality was to him. While he may not have understood it fully, he did get that I was never going to want a physical relationship.

How I figured out I was aromantic is a much shorter story. At first I identified as bi-romantic, since I still felt the same toward everyone—indifferent. Figuring out that I was aromantic took a lot less soul

[text obscured and illegible]

romantic attraction to anyone. It took a while and some more research, but now I think I've finally figured out my feelings. The love I feel toward people I care about is completely platonic or familial. The attraction I feel toward someone who I find attractive (e.g., Tom Hiddleston) is just aesthetic.

Looking back, it feels so obvious that I'm aro-ace (i.e., aromantic asexual). I sometimes wonder how my life would have changed if someone had explained these words to me in high school. If I knew the words, would I have identified as aro-ace immediately, or would I still have lived in denial for years? Who knows.

At the end of the day, I'm happy with how everything has turned out. I try not to dwell too much on how it could have been if I had known earlier that I'm aro-ace. Instead, I try to be as open as I can, posting information online, wearing my pride colors, participating in surveys—anything I can do to raise awareness and visibility of asexuality. I have even found a group of other asexual people in my area who meet up once a month. I have marched in my state's pride parade with my head held high, wearing my colors, and feeling accepted. I don't doubt my identity for a second; I'm truly happy and comfortable in my own skin. Now I can say with certainty that I'm not broken—I am aromantic and asexual, and proud of it!

Copper Weddings

Martin Spangsbro-Pedersen

Martin Spangsbro-Pedersen lives in Copenhagen, Denmark, where he works as a Controller. He is a long-time activist, and is engaged in different organizations within the LGBTQ+ community in Denmark, as well as a few feminist and anti-sexist projects. He has a blog, and collaborates with a few others on another blog detailing the lives of queer individuals in Denmark. He hopes to become a writer one day, and *Copper Weddings* is his first published piece.

year, I came out to the rest of my family and friends. 12 ½ years later, I "celebrated" by discarding the label I had used for myself. At the same time, I adopted a new one—asexual. And I found that this new label suited me far better than my former label had.

What happened was that, over the years, I felt my homosexual identity starting to become more restricting than liberating. A growing frustration took hold of me. I felt that everyone—myself included—had certain expectations for me, based on my sexual orientation. How I should act. How I should behave. What I should care about.

I wasn't the only one subjected to these expectations, of course, and I wasn't the only one trying to conform to them. But no one else seemed to mind these expectations but me. That, or it was just that no one talked about it.

I felt a pressure to behave a certain way so I could find acceptance. The times I didn't live up to these expectations, I felt others alienated me. But no matter what I did, my frustration wouldn't go away. In fact, it grew. I couldn't conform to the expectations, and it started to hurt me.

As my frustration grew, I gave it a name: "Broken." I felt broken, like something was wrong with me. I reasoned that, since everyone else seemed to be okay with these expectations, the problem had to lie with me. I was incomplete.

I lived with this feeling for quite some time. To help distract myself, I engaged in many projects within the LGBT community. One of these projects was the production of a dictionary with LGBTQ+ definitions, to which I became a major contributor.

Most of the work associated with this project was research. I became acquainted with sites about gender identities and sexual orientations—a lot of which I had never heard of before. Back when I was 19, there wasn't much of a choice when it came to orientation. You were either straight or gay. Bisexuality was a thing, too, but I associated it with people who were confused about themselves. (I want to point out that I don't think this way about bisexuality anymore.) Back then, though, I couldn't see myself as straight, so I had to be gay.

But, through my research, I found all these descriptions of orientations beside gay and straight. It broadened my perception of sexuality, which I'm thankful for. It caused me to start questioning my former beliefs on how you could identify your

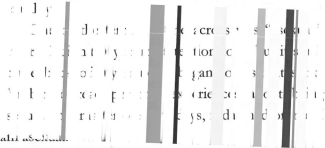

All of a sudden, the pieces fell into place. I watched as all the frustration I felt over my gay identity dissolved into thin air. I discovered that I fit much better into this new mold. It all made perfect sense. In that moment of realization, I left my broken

state completely. There was nothing wrong with me—other than the fact that I had been mislabeling myself all these years.

My adoption of a new identity happened without any hesitation or drama. In fact, it was over in the blink of an eye. I can't quite tell you why it was so easy for me. Maybe because I had felt uncomfortable with my other identity for some time? Still, it was a "Eureka!" moment, albeit a quiet one.

At first I was alone with this realization. I had a lot of stuff to figure out, so I didn't feel ready to talk to anyone about it. For example, I now understood my sexual orientation—but what about attraction? Were there different kinds of attraction, like there were different orientations? The more I learned, the more I analyzed my previous behavior and experiences to figure out how I functioned. What kind of attraction had I felt toward people before? Romantic, platonic, aesthetic—or a mix of these? There was so much I had to figure out before I could even begin to think about telling someone.

AVEN was one of the first sites I turned to. It helped me get into contact with others that felt the same as me. I learned a great deal about the issues of asexuality. Furthermore, it helped me understand the spectrum of asexuality better.

About a year passed, with me sucking up every piece of information I could find. I was able to finally answer the questions that filled my head, and I came out of the experience feeling like I understood myself much better than I had ever before.

One of the realizations I made was that I had mistaken my aesthetic attraction to people for romantic and/or sexual attraction. Furthermore, I had a thing for androgyny. Suddenly, I understood why I had mistaken my identity for gay. When I was a teenager, I felt attracted to certain guys about my own age or younger. At the time I thought it was a sexual attraction, but now I realize it had nothing to do with homosexuality—it was my aesthetic preference for androgyny that made them attractive.

With that sorted out, I started thinking a lot about my romantic preference. That was tricky for me to figure out, because I had difficulties separating [illegible]

[illegible] I wasn't coming closer to any form of truth. I settled with labeling myself as "questioning," or possibly "panromantic." These days if people ask, I will usually say I am panromantic. But I often add on: "At least for now." It seems easier to explain it that way, rather than tell them I am questioning. It works well for me right now. Will I identify like that later in life? I have no idea. Maybe I'll wake up one day and realize I'm (x)-romantic. Maybe I won't. Only time will tell.

Once I'd pinned down my orientation and romantic preference, I finally considered coming out to someone. I didn't feel an urge to tell the whole world—I just wanted someone to know about it. And I wanted the experience to be positive. So, I decided to tell someone within the LGBT/queer community where I volunteered, since a great number of people there already knew about the variety within sexual orientations.

I'm happy to say it went well. I admit I was somewhat afraid they would think less of me for not identifying as gay anymore. Luckily, that was never an issue. The few people I told were open-minded about it and had no problem accepting it. Some had questions about it and wanted to know more.

Within a few months, I must have told other people—that, or rumor started to spread. More people acknowledged my asexuality and started to ask me about it. One of my favorite "coming out" stories is when one of my friends guessed I was asexual without me even having to tell him. In the middle of the night after an evening out with friends, I got a text from him where he straight out asked if I was asexual. I did *not* see that coming. I knew he would be supportive, so I told him the truth and asked how he had known. His answer was two-fold. First, he claimed I give off some kind of asexual aura. Kind of a neat idea, one I'd never thought of before. Second, apparently I occasionally commented on things in a way that indicated my lack of interest in sex. For example, my friends would grumble about not having had sex for a week, or for a month, and I would say— with a smile—that I hadn't had sex in years. My friends would respond to comments like that with something along the lines of, "You don't care for sex anyway, so you don't count."

As it turned out, I'd been subconsciously dropping hints of my asexuality to my friends for years. Was that why they were so accepting of my asexuality? Did some of them see it coming before I

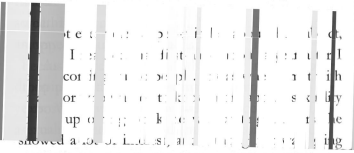

well. Then, after about an hour of me talking, he stopped me and said he had to ask me a question, because he couldn't make sense of something. He then proceeded to ask, very seriously, if I had been exposed to trauma as a child, or if I had been molested. I was taken aback, and at first I didn't know how to react. I hadn't seen this question coming. At all.

"No," was the short answer to his question. My childhood had been harmonious and quite happy, thanks very much.

The rest of our talk went quite well. But his question haunted me. Why would he associate childhood trauma with asexuality? I realized it was because he didn't understand how I felt and how I related to sex, so he was trying to rationalize it in a way that made sense to him. Of course, just as he couldn't understand me, I knew I would never be able to understand him and how he and other sexual people relate to sex. Our inability to understand each other was mutual.

This was the first, but not the last, time I would encounter a question like this. I realized I had been lucky that the people I confided in understood and supported me—other asexuals sometimes aren't that lucky.

Prejudice. That was the word that started to haunt me. My experience with the author was the first time I encountered prejudice toward asexuality, and his words had burned themselves into my mind. How should I deal with it the next time it happened? What should I say?

I already knew a few things about dealing with prejudice, but I had no idea how to counter it. So I started researching again, and found a lot of great things along the way. I found accounts of asexual people who had encountered prejudice, and I was able to draw on their experiences and thoughts on the subject. I also began reading about asexuality in more academic terms. It helped me get a better idea of what I was up against.

Explaining something outside of mainstream society, like asexuality, is a difficult task. Not an impossible one, but difficult. Everything in western culture works on the assumption that everyone is interested in sex. It has been ingrained in us that every human being experiences sexual attraction to others. Everyone wants to have sex, and everyone pursues it.

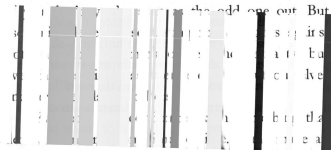

effort to understand. But most don't, and they often try to disprove what they don't understand, going under the assumption that there's something wrong with it. That was exactly how the author reacted. He failed to understand what I was saying to him, and his way of making sense of it was to assume I'm asexual only because I had been hurt in a way that "broke" me. Made me incomplete. In his mind, he probably equates someone who has sex as being "healthy"—therefore, as someone who doesn't have or want sex, I must by default be "unhealthy." He saw me as someone in need of fixing—someone who isn't actually asexual, but just hasn't yet reached their full (sexual) potential.

This not only frustrated me, but enraged me. Now I can see how I could have given the author a much better answer than the one I gave him. Hopefully one day I'll get the chance. Until then, I can only practice answering questions like this, because chances are I'll encounter them again. But this time I come prepared! Prepared to answer, but also to criticize the structures of our society and the expectations that everyone is supposed to live up to. Expectations that hurt so many people, especially those who can't live up to them.

The author's question ignited a spark in me—a passion for activism, to do something about the way most people see asexuality. The spark has only grown since then. I am a firm believer in visibility projects and believe that—if framed right—they can make a positive difference. Not only to all the sexual people who don't understand or believe in asexuality, but, most importantly, to everyone who right now believes they are "broken."

Right before I had this meeting with the author, I got a request to attend a workshop and speak about my asexuality. The workshop was with counselors in the national LGBT organization—they wanted to educate themselves on the subject of asexuality. As it turned out, I was the only asexual person they knew, which is why they asked me. At first, I wasn't sure whether or not to accept the invitation—but, after meeting with the author, I decided to attend. I needed to start somewhere, after all. And I'm pleased to say it went well. They were open-minded, and really made an effort to understand what I was telling them. We had many great reflections throughout the session.

That was about a year ago. Since then, I've ⬛⬛⬛ for ⬛⬛⬛ about visibility ⬛⬛⬛ help ⬛ a few ⬛ the ⬛ people I've begun ⬛⬛⬛ this ⬛⬛⬛ que⬛ community to as⬛ ⬛⬛⬛ al ⬛ s⬛lity ⬛ Outside of ⬛ ⬛ rrn⬛, I e c t⬛ two ⬛ n lectures an⬛ ⬛ c s o c ⬛ x⬛ ien ⬛ sometimes ⬛ audience professional ⬛ ⬛ c ⬛⬛ors, and other times young people (below the age of 25). I've also volunteered for interviews on research papers, school projects, and projects made by people studying to become journalists. Furthermore, I've assisted others and helped form an asexual community here in Copenhagen.

I'm satisfied with most of what I've done so far. A few experiences turned out badly, due to misunderstandings and my inability to articulate my points as precisely as I envisioned them in my head. Other discussions drowned in prejudiced questions and opinions. I have made mistakes, but I have learned from these. I hope I continue to improve.

I do all this because I want to make a difference. If my activism can somehow make a positive difference for someone who right now believes themselves to be "broken," then I have reached my goal. In fact, I'm sure that would only fuel my drive to engage myself further in this work.

12 ½ years of marriage forms a copper wedding. My first copper wedding—adopting my gay identity—was a great experience, but it left me thinking I was "broken," and that something was wrong with me. The marriage became toxic and restricted me in a great many ways. I found a new "lover" in asexuality, and discarded my old relationship. It was the greatest thing I could ever have done for myself. Today, I feel like a new, whole person, and I'm much more aware of my relations to other people. I can now recognize and navigate the different ways I'm attracted to people. I've learned so

much the last few years, and I hope that journey isn't over yet.

And who knows? In 9 ½ years I might discover something new about myself and celebrate another copper wedding. In the meantime, though, I hope this marriage is going to be a much more enjoyable one than my last.

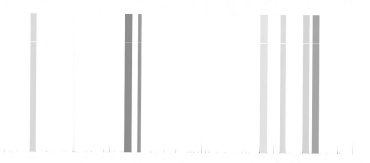

My Happily Ever After
Cecily Summers

Cecily Summers is a 20-something Canadian writer who enjoys all things science fiction and fantasy.

I've always loved Disney movies. When I was a kid, I used to dream of how my own romance would unfold—I'd meet an amazing guy, we'd fall in love, maybe sing a few songs along the way, and then we'd ride off into the sunset and live happily ever after. Then I hit puberty and discovered that "living happily ever after" with someone typically involved a lot of making out and groping and licking and grinding of bodies together in a hot, sweaty mess. And, suddenly, I was no longer quite as eager to find my Prince Charming.

My first experience with dating was in the eighth grade. Back then, I didn't know much about sex—all I really understood was that if a girl and a boy liked each other, they would go on a date, hold hands, and kiss. The problem was that I didn't want to kiss any of the boys I knew. Sure, I enjoyed hanging out with them—and, yes, I did get a happy little flutter in my heart when a cute boy laughed at my joke or complimented me—but I had no particular urge to kiss them.

Since girls my age were definitely supposed to want to kiss boys, I assumed I was just a late bloomer. Given enough exposure to boys in romantic situations, I was sure my interest in kissing and dating would grow accordingly. So, when a cute boy asked me out on a movie date, I gathered up my courage, pushed aside that nagging voice in my head telling me it wasn't what I wanted, and accepted the invitation.

It turned out to be a group outing, which made the pre-show part much easier; with a bunch of friends around, I didn't have to worry about my date trying anything too intimate with me. Then the movie started, and suddenly there I was, sitting beside a boy in a dark theater, unable to enjoy or even pay a_t_ion _o t__ __ b___ __ I __ev __a a_ __ __i_ __ _ight gra_ __ __a_ __ __ap hi_ __n __r_u_ __ __ s__ders or __ — ___ __ kiss __e

__'s _ot l__ I __ __t _y __g ha__ __u_ h__ n as _ resu__ __ _ __ __ i_c_ d__ u__nfor_abl_ __ h__ __ a o __hi __ __li__in __e A_ __ yes, a_ __ par_ _f my __e__ __a_ _irs_ _a__ jitters, combined with a healthy dosage of social awkwardness and shyness. But, deep down, I didn't *want* to be kissed. Because even though I had only the vaguest understanding of sex, I knew that kissing wasn't just kissing—it always led to something else, something more. And I didn't want that something more, even if I didn't really understand what it was.

I was proud of myself afterward for successfully going on my first-ever date—another life experience to check off my list!—but it was overall a nerve-wracking and unenjoyable evening. We continued "dating" for a few months after that, barely seeing each other outside of school. I didn't really want to be dating him, but he was nice, he seemed to like me, and I enjoyed the way my social standing rose now that I "had a boyfriend," so I stuck it out. After we broke up, I decided the problem had been twofold: I was too young, shy, and nervous to be dating, and he just wasn't the right guy for me.

A few years passed, and soon I was in high school. When my friends asked why I didn't have a boyfriend, I'd tell them it was because I was busy with school, or clubs, or family activities, or whatever excuse I could come up with on the spot. When they pried further, I'd admit to maybe finding so-and-so cute—which wasn't a lie, as I have a great aesthetic appreciation for attractive men. But when they suggested I actually do something about my crush— i.e., ask him out—I immediately changed the subject. I had no problem determining who was cute and who was not; I just had no interest in dating them.

It's not like I didn't get the appeal of dating. I loved the idea of having a guy around who wanted nothing more than to hang out with you, be there for you, give you gifts, and make you laugh. But then I would see my friends pressed up against lockers making out with their boyfriends, hands all over each other, clothing askew, and I'd think, "That looks exhausting. It just goes on and on and on. If that's what's required to have a boyfriend, I'll pass."

I mean, I understood that kissing was supposed to be amazing and mind-blowing, hence why people did it all the time. I understood that when you saw your crush in the hallway, or when you accidentally brushed fingers while passing each other, you were supposed to get all tingly and warm inside. And, sure, I did feel gooey and romantic when I watched the hero kiss his leading lady on the big screen. I just balked at the idea of experiencing those things for

m   e   r   s   n   y   asn t

]   r e   l   , I   s i   u d o h

c   c h   7. t t   I e sl

c i   v   t   vas l s   I o k n

a   t w   c e ut, e   u l

fc c e t   ut   d r

it   n   w tched *Star Wars*, it was Han Solo I swooned over, not Princess Leia. Did that mean I was bisexual? But I felt no desire to be intimate with either sex. So if I wasn't straight, gay, or bi … what was I?

I kept my questions to myself. I don't like talking about my feelings. Never have, never will. I really wish I had talked to someone, though, because looking back it's pretty obvious I was depressed throughout high school. My mother asked me a few times if I was all right, and I always laughed off her concerns and insisted I was fine. I wasn't, of course, but I didn't want to burden her with my problems—especially not when I didn't even understand what my problems were.

You have to remember that, at the time, I had no idea asexuality existed. I just figured there was something fundamentally screwed up in my brain that was preventing me from having a normal, healthy interest in dating. I thought of my apathy toward acquiring a boyfriend not as "just the way I am," but as something I absolutely had to fix if I ever wanted to be a happy, functioning member of society.

Because I spent my teenage years thinking there was something wrong with me, I had very low self-confidence and felt an extreme lack of self-worth. And since I couldn't figure out what was wrong with me, I was left with this feeling that I was somehow inferior to other people—that they deserved to have more than me because they were willing and able to experience life more fully than I was.

Finally, I reached university. In my freshman year, I covered all the basics—got drunk for the first time, pulled an all-nighter, skipped class, went to a house party, and so on. The only thing I didn't do was date. By that point, I'd decided that the only way I was going to successfully have a boyfriend was if I found "the one"—the guy who I'd fall in love with at first sight, who would make all my unease and confusion and insecurities melt away, and everything in my life would finally click perfectly into place.

In second year I didn't find "the one," but I did get a boyfriend. I tend to force myself to do things I don't want to do in an attempt to make sure I'm not missing out on anything. It's almost as if I view life as a video game—if I complete the quest "Go on a date," I get experience points and level up as a human being. Which ties back into the whole self-worth thing—if I've leveled up, it means I'm living life more [illegible] he asked me out, I said yes. I didn't find him particularly attractive, but hey, he liked me, and he wanted to date me, so why not give it a shot? Worst case scenario, it wouldn't work out and we'd break up—but at least I'd get some valuable dating experience that I could use when I did eventually find "the one."

I'm oversimplifying, of course. I was terrified of dating him, since I was very aware that having a college boyfriend meant sex was inevitable. I guess I was just hoping he'd awaken some dormant passion in me that would make me actually want to try having sex. As you can probably guess, that didn't happen.

It was the same story as grade eight all over again. I enjoyed hanging out with him in group settings, because it was more-or-less platonic—he lavished attention on me, and laughed at my jokes, and was just fun in general to be around. But when we were alone, I wanted to be anywhere but there. We would lie on his bed, kissing and groping—always instigated by him, of course—and instead of being inflamed with passion, I was mostly just bored. I also felt incredibly awkward, because my kissing technique was laughably lackluster and mainly consisted of copying exactly what he did. I had no idea if I was doing it right, since all it felt like to me was mashing my lips randomly against his.

I broke up with him after a few months, as I didn't want to lead him on when there was obviously nothing there. He was upset by the breakup, but I was incredibly relieved. Once again, I figured the problem had to be that A) there was still something wrong with me, and B) he wasn't the right guy. Because when you kiss "the one," you definitely aren't bored. You don't lie there while he gropes your chest and kisses your neck and think, "There are so many other, more interesting things I could be doing right now." You don't flush crimson when he says, "You know, you don't have to be so quiet when I'm kissing you," because you know you're supposed to be moaning and panting with barely-contained lust, but all you feel is vaguely uncomfortable.

So, yeah. Breaking up was definitely the right decision.

Six months later, I finally met the perfect guy. He was cute, and funny, and sweet, and we got along amazingly. So, when he started flirting with me, I flirted back as best as I could. I thought to myself, "This is it. This is the guy. This is the most attracted I' _ er_ t _ r_ _, _ _ i _ g _ _ o k_ _ a c , i _ _ l _ _ " _ _ l _ t, s id _ s. a _ s d _ _

_ta_ _w_ _ i_ _ _ _ _ _ f _ _ _ _, e_ _ _ l_ _ _ _ _ g t _ _ _ n _ _ _ _ w d _a _ s _ _ _ _ _ _ _ _ _ _ p _ s _ _ _ _ f _ _ _ me nc _ _ _ intimate with him, hoping that eventually I would start wanting him the way he wanted me. One thing led to another, and I told him I was ready to have sex. The foreplay was kind of nice, but when we got to the actual insert-part-A-into-part-B ... nothing. No flood of desire. No overwhelming passion. Just some pain—I was a virgin—and an overwhelming desire for the boring and awkward experience to end. Which it soon did, as he quickly picked up that I simply wasn't into it.

Even though he assured me that everything was fine, and not to worry about what had happened, and that our brief and prematurely aborted tryst definitely counted as "having sex"—another life experience to check off the list!—I still felt humiliated. And guilty, since it had been his first time, too. Had I ruined it for him? I hadn't meant to. What was wrong with me, that I didn't seem to want or enjoy sex at all?

That was a really hard conversation to have with myself, believe you me. And I had no solid answers. I even turned to the internet for help. "Why don't I like having sex?" The most common reason I could find was that people who disliked sex tended to have experienced some sort of childhood trauma or abusive relationship. But nothing of the sort had happened to me.

So if my problem wasn't emotional or mental, was it physical? I went to the doctor and asked for a full check-up, hoping they would notice something amiss in my bloodwork that would explain my bizarre disinclination toward sex. But they found nothing wrong with me, so I was back to square one.

A few weeks later, my boyfriend showed up at my front door. After a long conversation—during which he was tactful enough not to bring up our botched attempt at sex—we mutually parted ways. Unlike my previous two breakups, this one definitely hurt. As I said, I loved hanging out with this guy, and a breakup meant I wouldn't see him around very much. But the main thing I felt was relief. Single again!

That was the turning point. I had finally found the perfect guy, and still it hadn't worked. I started to realize that it had nothing to do with who I was dating—it had to do with me. For whatever reason, I just didn't want to be in a sexual relationship. And yes, that inspired yet more feelings of confusion and self-loathing. I managed to distract myself from those feelings by hanging out with friends, reading books, and watching TV, but they were always there at the back of my mind, nagging at the conviction that I was an animal who would rather be tidy and up.

A couple of years ago, I stumbled across the "asexuality" which immediately something that intrigued me. I suspected had to be right, apply to me, but I rejected the idea instead. For reason I felt, by accepting that identity, I was swearing an oath to myself that I would never have sex again. Which wouldn't be a problem at all, except for the fact that deep down in my heart I still dreamed about finding my Prince Charming. And considering how overly-sexualized our society is—I'm sure you've heard the oft-quoted tidbit: "Men think about sex every seven seconds"—I was convinced that adopting an asexual identity and admitting I didn't desire sex was basically ensuring my own sad, lonely ending.

A few months later, I came across AVEN's website. I was once again hit by the terrifying thought that I would die alone and unloved. Then I gathered my courage and started to read through the various posts. And, gradually, everything became clear.

Asexuality isn't a life sentence for unhappiness—it's the complete opposite, actually. I learned there were thousands of asexual people out there leading happy, healthy, loving lives—some in relationships with sexual people, some in relationships with other asexual people, and some single by choice and perfectly content. And I realized that if they were all able to find their happily ever afters, there's no reason I wouldn't be able to do so as well.

That was the real turning point. Once I embraced my asexuality, my entire outlook on life changed. Suddenly, I didn't think of myself as abnormal or broken. I stopped believing there was something wrong with me that was preventing me from finding happiness. It was as if I'd been living with a terminal disease my entire life, and had suddenly found a cure. That may sound a bit melodramatic, but it's really how I felt.

I used to laugh at people who walked around wearing t-shirts with inspirational phrases like "Know Thyself" written on them. I thought they were snooty and pretentious. But I don't laugh at them anymore. Knowing myself, and understanding why I am the way I am, has changed everything. It's made me feel worthwhile, made me feel like I can try harder and care more because finally—finally!—I actually feel like I belong.

I've come pretty far since I was that little girl dreaming of Prince Charming and fairy tale endings. It's been quite a journey, and not one I'd particularly care to repeat. But I'm glad I took it, because even though I haven't found my happily ever after yet, at least now I have a better idea of what I'm looking for. And what I'm *not* looking for.

Conclusion

A.K. Andrews

As you've seen through this collection of stories, asexuality is not an easy road to walk. Most people don't even know it exists, which makes identifying as asexual and coming out as asexual a difficult task indeed. But thanks to Tumblr, AVEN, asexual activists, and projects like this one, we're getting there. It's a slow process, but not a thankless one—because helping someone realize they're not broken, that they're simply an orientation they've never heard of before, is one of the most satisfying feelings in the world.

If you're interested in contributing to asexual visibility and awareness, there are many ways to do so. You can click your way over to the AVEN website and find out more about asexuality, and about what you can do to help. You can blog about it, tell your friends, tell your teachers, march in a pride parade … basically, share your knowledge of asexuality in any way that works for you.

If you'd like to participate in a future *Ace and Proud* anthology, contact us at our email address (purplecakepress@gmail.com) and let us know you'd like to share a story or poem in the next volume.

You can also keep an eye on our website (purplecakepress.wordpress.com) for more details about upcoming projects.

And, now, it's "thank you" time!

Thank you to the wonderful writers who were kind and courageous enough to share their stories with me. Working with you has been a genuine pleasure, and I wish you all the luck in the world with your future endeavors.

Thank you to Victoria Beth from the AVEN Project Team for writing such a beautiful foreword. You captured the spirit of this project perfectly, and I couldn't have asked for a better introduction to the anthology.

Finally, thank you to *you,* dear reader, for purchasing this book! Whatever your reason for buying

—you never know whose life you might change for the better!

Live long and prosper, my friends. And above all else, be true to yourself.

Made in the USA
Monee, IL
18 January 2022